EATING
AT WORK

Ishi Khosla
& Nina Mehta

EATING AT WORK

Practice the five 'Ps' to achieve peak performance

Ishi Khosla
& Nina Mehta

SIMON &
SCHUSTER

London • New York • Sydney • Toronto • New Delhi

A CBS COMPANY

First published in India by Simon & Schuster India, 2019
A CBS company

Copyright © Ishi Khosla, 2019

The right of Ishi Khosla to be identified as author of
this work has been asserted by her in accordance with
Section 57 of the Copyright Act 1957.

1 3 5 7 9 10 8 6 4 2

Simon & Schuster India
818, Indraprakash Building,
21, Barakhamba Road,
New Delhi 110001

www.simonandschuster.co.in

Paperback ISBN: 978-93-86797-34-6
eBook ISBN: 978-93-86797-35-3

Typeset in India by Mridu Agarwal, Simon & Schuster, New Delhi

Printed and bound in India by Replika Press Pvt. Ltd.

DISCLAIMER: Information and views expressed in this manual are based on
clinical experience of the authors and scientific research. It does not replace
medical opinion or treatment.

CONTENTS

FOREWORD

Eating at Work by Ishi Khosla is an important, timely book that gives excellent advice and suggestions on following the right diet for everyone, especially professionals, who often find it difficult to inculcate healthy eating habits at the workplace because of stress, irregular timings and other work related problems.

Food is an essential part of health and well-being and eating safe and nutritious food is an enabler for a happier, healthier life. Ishi Khosla, a clinical nutritionist, understands this better than most people. The book effectively addresses this need, provides detailed information and guidelines on how to manage one's weight and diet, not through quick starvation diets that don't provide any long term benefits, but through easy, lifestyle changes that will help you eat right.

I recommend this book for every professional including those struggling with weight and health problems – simply to improve one's lifestyle and habits in a manner that adds value to your life.

FSSAI (Food Safety and Standards Authority of India, Ministry of Health and Family Welfare, Government of India) has recently launched an 'Eat Right' movement and we are delighted that Ishi Khosla has written a book that perfectly fits our thoughts and ideas on safe and nutritious eating at the workplace.

Please do read this book and support the 'Eat Right' movement to promote and enable a healthier, happier future for the citizens of our nation.

Pawan Agarwal, IAS
Secretary (GoI) and Chief Executive Officer (FSSAI)

INTRODUCTION

Poor diet is responsible for more deaths globally than tobacco, high blood pressure, or any other health risk, according to a new scientific study; yet we don't pay attention to what we eat, when we eat and how we eat.

- Dr Ashkan Afshin, Head of *Global Burden of Disease Project*

Keeping in mind the fact that most of the busy professionals are devoting more than half of their waking hours to work – be it office, outside or even at home, expecting them to be mindful of what they eat is a tall order. Not only are they multi-tasking but are perpetually stressed and fueled by an adrenaline rush. And in such a state nothing is more comforting than food. Emotional eating is often the result of this kind of work pressure. No matter how much information one has, it takes a lot for any busy person to manage their food. Either they forget to eat or binge or they constantly crave sugary high carbohydrate and high fat foods. More often these are foods which have addictive properties, containing caffeine, sugar and wheat. Most processed foods are designed chemically to make them addictive. The caffeine high and sugar rush are so familiar. The obvious consequences range from weight gain, belly fat, to digestive disorders and skin issues like acne, hair fall and dandruff. Eventually these disorders take the shape of diseases like thyroid disorders, diabetes, high blood pressure, joint pains and deficiency disorders including anemia and osteoporosis, to name a few. These I see every day in my clinic.

There is no point in simply saying NO. We cannot give people only information about foods or ask them to be mindful when the environment is not controlled. Healthy eating at work has to be a holistic approach else we add another burden on already stressed minds. Non-compliance to dietary wisdom will make them feel like failures and ridden with guilt. So we need to have a workplace which provides or serves healthier alternatives – salads, fruits (Refer to *Read more,* page 314), vegetables, nuts, seeds, soups, etc. We need to restrict serving deep fried snacks like samosas and trans-fat laden biscuits in meetings and instead serve nuts, seeds and roasted snacks. In lieu of premix beverages, workplaces must serve infusion teas and options of unsweetened teas / coffees. Employers need to take responsibility to make the workplace safer and healthier. Food safety is closely related to people's lives, health, economic development and social harmony.

Simply put, we need to sensitize our workplace. The Chinese government in fact took it upon itself, more than a decade ago, to provide healthy food options in all government institutions. FSSAI in India has launched the first of its kind healthy workplace initiative — The "Eat right movement" across the country. It is a nation-wide campaign to help people eat safe, eat healthy and eat right at their work place. Several multinational offices also have responded to the growing burden in obesity and diseases by offering healthier food options. Combine this with simple understanding of foods and some simple rules to follow, one can help the busiest professionals navigate different, often challenging, situations.

Diet rules should be such that they become your life partners quite literally – travel with you, party with you and celebrate with you. Don't we all know that there is no love more sincere than the love of food. So embrace healthy eating and love your food.

This book aims to help by being a quick, easy-to-read guide. It offers actionable strategies and practical tips to professionals under different working conditions. It will not take away the pleasure of eating, in fact it teaches you simple ways of eating your favourite foods. Having said that it is difficult to oversimplify food choices which are steeped in cultural diversity and unique health and taste preferences. While you arm yourselves with the knowledge that is provided here, never let go off your best tools – common sense, instinct and logic. This book comes as a unique manual and its relevance for our workforce can hardly be overemphasized.

A healthy nation is indeed a wealthy nation.

As Mahatma Gandhi said 'It is health which is real wealth, and not pieces of gold and silver.'

Eating at work is a book, written to bring over 25 years

of clinical practice and research out of my office and into everyone's workplace and everyday lives. As a practicing integrative nutritionist, I have presented the science and art of eating in diverse work situations keeping simple food facts and principles in mind.

The five Ps devised in this book, together with a few tips, make a complete tool bag to keep our body and mind powerful today, tomorrow, and over a lifetime.

COMMON WORKPLACE DISASTERS

Sveta is feeling on top of the world. Her first week at the telecom MNC has been a success, as has been her move to the millennium city, Gurugram. Now she wants to figure out how to lose a few kilos, deal with polycystic ovaries and acne, and she will be a happy 24-year old.

Srikumar is running late for the case he is defending at the Supreme Court. To make it in time for the hearing he will have to skip lunch, nothing new for this 35-year-old lawyer. But yesterday's visit to the doctor was a warning bell – if he doesn't regulate his eating, he will end up popping pills to be in shape and keep diseases away.

Rushing back home to shower and change, Sandeep is anxious and is busy going over the pitch he will make to the client he is meeting over dinner. It has to be the right mix of business and fun. The client's weakness is Italian cuisine and Sandeep has made a reservation at one of the best Italian restaurants in town, even though the huge snack he had an hour ago after missing lunch, still sits heavy in his stomach.

Did he eat breakfast? Never mind, he thinks, keeping the antacid in his pocket.

Checklist. Facebook and Twitter updated, Instagram update, Morning Bell track, en route office. Akhtar grabs an apple that his doctor has recommended – for his bowels. What a problem to have, sighs Akhtar, can't even get sympathy votes! To top it all, he has to pop pills to keep a regular bowel movement.

That pretty much sums up the eating habits of urban office-goers. People are found at two ends of the spectrum – snacking continuously or taking long gaps between meals or skipping meals. They not only eat whatever they get, but they eat whenever they get it. And years of this senseless and thoughtless eating leads to hair fall, skin disorders, digestive issues, heartburn, constipation, stress, anxiety, a foggy mind, mood swings, attention deficit disorders, depression, polycystic ovaries etc. These are a precursor to obesity, high blood pressure, pre-diabetes, abnormal cholesterol levels, and even autoimmune disorders. Our diet is important, perhaps more important today than it ever was, given the epidemic of lifestyle-related diseases. All of us, especially those who are away at work or deal with high-pressure jobs paired with erratic schedules, need to take cognizance of what we eat, how we eat, how much we eat, when we eat and most importantly how we digest it. There is no escape from the consequences!

And then there are those who are trying hard to practice smart eating and exercising but not quite successful in getting results. Through better understanding of their bodies and getting to the root cause of their problems, they can surely transform their lives through the right food.

FOOD – THE TICKING TIME BOMB

At the workplace all stakeholders put food at the bottom of their list of priorities. Ever so often the workplace meal programmers are either an afterthought or are completely non-existent.

Workplace cafeterias or food courts are often stocked with calorie-dense foods high in fat, sugar and salt, leaving the consumers with limited or without healthy options. Many employers believe that adults are responsible for their own health. Sometimes, employees feel pressurized to skip lunch due to deadlines leading to desktop dining or SAD (stuck at desk) phenomenon.

Both overlook a nuance that skipping meal(s) lowers productivity, increases stress and leads to unhealthy snacking. The quality of what we eat and drink at work directly impacts the quality of work and productivity. Snacking on sugary foods and drinks which the body quickly digests leads to an instant surge in energy but ultimately leaves the body more tired – not to forget the growing waistlines and piling kilos.

Numerous studies indicate that food at work may impact

not only employee health but also impact the company's health. International Labour Organization (ILO), since its inception in 1919, has defined key elements of proper nutrition, demonstrating the link between poor nutrition and poor output, and the link between good nutrition and good output* (Christopher Wanjak, 2005, Food at Work: Workplace Solutions for Malnutrition, Obesity and Chronic Diseases, International Labour Organisation, Geneva).

The connection between nutrition, fatigue and drowsiness is well known. Fatigue or lack of energy often reflects overwork or a nutritional deficiency, which is most commonly iron, but also B vitamins. Iron deficiency is the most common nutritional disorder in the world (about 80% of the world's population may have some level of iron deficiency). Besides sluggishness, it results in low immunity, low endurance and as much as 30% decrease in work productivity for mental and physical tasks.

The common workplace disasters listed below illustrate that apathy towards food is a ticking time bomb.

SKIP BREAKFAST

We all know the importance of eating breakfast yet 'breakfast skipping' is an emerging pattern. It could be due to shortage of time or poor management but the result is shortage of nutrition. Some do not eat at all but down cups of tea/coffee and biscuits to keep the engine running resulting in nutritional deficiencies or digestive disorders. Most nutritional guidelines recommend that you eat breakfast daily and that by skipping it you are increasing the risk of obesity as well as numerous chronic diseases.

A meta-analysis in 2019 with 6000 plus participants showed that breakfast skipping is associated with an increased risk of type 2 diabetes, partly because of increase in obesity.

After six to ten hours of fasting due to sleep, during which the blood sugar levels

> Possible effects of Skipping Breakfast
> ·Drop in blood sugar levels
> ·Slow metabolic rate
> ·Increase in stress hormones
> ·Increased risk of chronic diseases

are maintained by the liver through the breakdown of glycogen (the stored form of glucose) and the synthesis of glucose from amino acids (building blocks of proteins), breakfast provides energy and replenishes glucose stores. By ignoring and not replenishing the glucose levels you will end up feeling overly hungry, irritable and fatigued during the better part of the day.

For many, also eating the morning breakfast has become 'desk-fast' – it is partaken at the desk. Coupled with passive work habits, long hours at the desk and stress may lead to rapid weight gain and associated health problems. However, not everyone is hungry in the morning. If one is not hungry then a light snack comprising of eggs, sprouts, nuts, fruits, vegetables, milk, vegetable juices or smoothies is a good option. It is difficult to eat a full meal if one is not hungry. Breaking a fast with light food is prudent. With the popularity of a new diet pattern called intermittent fasting (Refer to *Read more*, page 273) many are skipping this meal altogether.

DASHBOARD DINING

Dashboard (Grab-n-Go) dining is defined as any food or drink consumed in the car, whether you are driving or being driven. Eating while driving is becoming a common practice as the time spent on the road has increased. Besides the safety aspect it is found that the foods consumed while 'snacking on the go' usually have high and unhealthy calories.

SUGAR AND CAFFEINE KICK-START

(Refer to *Read more*, page 226)

A workplace is not complete without tea or coffee. The caffeine kick is a must when you enter office. It is also synonymous with 'drive and focus' at work. For many the habit begins as a break from the monotony of sitting at a desk, or the desire to eat something between meals. At times the reason to drink coffee can be unique. A gentleman I met in Finland confessed drinking one litre of coffee simply because he felt entitled to as he did not drink alcohol (Refer to *Read more*, page 244) or smoke! Of late, green tea and green coffee and cold brewed coffee (Refer to *Read more*, page 226) also included in this category of beverages. The concerns here are not tea and coffee per se but the caffeine and sugar which is gulped down with each cup.

Drink	Serving size (ml)	Caffeine content (mg)
Coffee(drip method)	150	115
Coffee (percolator)	150	80
Instant coffee	150	65
Tea	150	40
Espresso	30	40
Decaffeinated coffee	150	03
Cold brew	150	60

FOOD COMA

Many people struggle to concentrate for about an hour or two after a lunch break. Feeling sleepy, lethargic, drowsy or fatigued after meals is common and is referred to as 'food coma' or 'carb coma', also called 'postprandial somnolence'. As the name suggests 'postprandial' means after a meal and 'somnolence' means a strong desire to sleep or a feeling of drowsiness.

Wisdom that has been passed down through generations:
·You are what you eat
· Chew your food well
· Eat at the table

It may also be accompanied with extreme fullness, bloating, mental fogginess, difficulty in concentration and reduced attention span. While this sleepiness may not be confined to the middle of the day, a study published in the Journal of Applied Physiology in 1998 reported that the extent of the postprandial sleepiness was greatest after meals eaten between 11.00 am and 2.00 pm.

THE DEVIL'S HOURS (5-7 CHAOS)

According to diet recalls, most people trying to eat smart, manage well until evening. Hunger peaks between 5-7 pm for most, leading to consumption of unhealthy food, snacks and extra calories, and therein starts the chaos of the devil's hours.

Food certainly provides great comfort and is a perfect partner to de-stress with, thereby, also becoming an internal stimulus to eat. Whether it is physiological or psychological is hard to distinguish. Perhaps it is both.

So compelling is the need to eat, that many grab the first thing they can reach out to which is more often than not oily, starchy and processed snacks – fried namkeens, chips, biscuits, samosas, pakoras, pizzas, noodles, sandwiches etc. Worse still, this could be followed by a few drinks paired with snacks ending with a hearty dinner, topped up with a favourite dessert close to midnight. This is nothing but a recipe for disaster.

Such food extravaganza not only increases the caloric

intake, it also loads up the system at the wrong time resulting in digestive disturbances including hyper-acidity, gastritis, constipation, irritable bowel syndrome (IBS), fatigue, sleep disturbances and expanding waistlines. Unchecked, this eventually results in metabolic changes like dyslipidemia (high blood cholesterol levels), high blood pressure, increased uric acid leading eventually to diabetes and heart disease. It also sets the stage for auto-immune disorders. Research shows that eating late into the night can disturb hormonal balances.

I have patients who were eating dinner by 7:00–7:30 pm and were losing weight. Then they shifted their dinner to 9 pm. Then they stopped losing and on the contrary gained weight and inches on the waist. So almost the same calories but eaten at a different time simply demonstrates that a calorie is not just a calorie!

NIGHT SHIFTS

Erratic work hours alter the circadian rhythms and change bodily functions. Circadian is a Latin word meaning 'around a day'. Circadian rhythms are regular mental and physical changes that occur during a day. The most well-known circadian rhythm is the human sleep cycle. Disturbed circadian rhythms adversely affect body weight, temperature, metabolism, blood pressure, hormones (cortisol, growth hormone, insulin, melatonin (Refer to *Read more,* page 255), leptin), leading to digestive disturbances, compromised immunity, low mental alertness, skin and hair health, to name a few.

Altered circadian rhythms along with the consumption of high calorie, oil laden, high salt high sugar and dangerous trans-fats-loaded snack food from vending machines or cafeterias, long gaps between meals, over the top partying, drinking, smoking, stress and no exercise is a lethal cocktail. The outcome can range from minor complaints like increased infections, flu, sleeping disturbances, menstrual disorders (PCOS — Refer to *Read more*, page 257), fatigue, heartburn, constipation, IBS (irritable bowel syndrome), bloating, flatulence to serious ones like obesity, hypertension (high blood pressure), heart disease, diabetes, infertility and many more. A cab driver I met in Dubai said he had gained 10 kgs in a year ever since he shifted his day time job to night shifts while eating the same food. While he was making more money he was certainly losing his health. This represents almost all those working against the clock and the need to prevent this phenomena by better understanding and diet management.

LONG WORKING HOURS

Working long hours can have detrimental effects on health — from increased stress to higher rates of certain chronic disease like diabetes. In a large study exploring the effect of extended work hours researchers from the institute for work and health in Toronto analyzed data of more than 7,000 workers in Canada who were followed for more than 12 years to understand whether work hours can effect the risk of diabetes. They reported that women working more than

45 hours a week had a 51% higher risk of developing diabetes during the study period compared to women working 35 to 40 hours a week. (That was after the scientists adjusted for other potential factors that could affect diabetes risk, including physical activity, BMI and smoking.).

OFFICE PARTIES

Offices instead of facilitating or even accommodating healthy food choices become a hindrance. Even my most disciplined clients trying to lose weight seem to give in to pressures of eating at office. The aroma of samosas, bread pakoras, patties, paranthas, burgers, pizzas and the sight of cakes, pastries or gulab jamuns leads to loss of control, despite no intentions of eating. This is when the senses take over the mind – happens to the best of us, but when it becomes a regular affair, it's time to think! Since, almost every day is a celebration in office with birthdays, meetings and occasions, it's a good idea to evaluate 'office party' foods. So, next time plan your office party around smart foods, prepared from whole grains, fruits, vegetables, nuts and seeds.

Considering that employees spend the better part of their day (half of their waking hours) at work, workplace represents a logical place to ensure proper nutrition. When companies run initiatives that provide healthy food choices with fruit and vegetable breaks and access to physical activity, employees have reported a change in their eating preferences, many have lost weight and now look forward to healthier food options.

FOOD – AN ADDICTION: CONTROLS PLEASURES & MOODS

ADDICTIVE FOODS

A smoker(Refer to *Read more*, page 252), alcoholic (Refer to *Read more*, page 244) or any other substance abuser knows that addiction damages the body. But no matter how hard they try, cutting back is rarely successful. It has to be an all or none rule. The addictive substance has to be completely eliminated for a reasonable length of time to get de-addicted. It is quite appropriate and no exaggeration to say that certain foods may have the same addictive effects on us.

Besides caffeine, the two most addictive foods in our

Smart Snacking Options

SNACKS

· Poha with peanuts & vegetables

· Idli / Dosa with chutney

· Roti rolls with vegetables/ paneer/ egg/ chicken

· Falafel/ Vegetable kebabs / tikkis

· Crackers & chips with dips

· Dhokla & khandavi

· Thin-crust pizzas

· Multigrain bread sandwiches

· Multigrain Bhel

· Roasted khakhra

· Carrot, radish & cucumber sticks (with or without dips)

· Sprouts (Refer to *Read more*, page 266)

· Salads with low calorie dressings

· Yogurt/raita with fruits & vegetables

· Roasted whole grains like channa, pulses or lentils

· Roasted nuts

current diets happen to be sugar and wheat.

Studies have found sugar to be several times more addictive than cocaine, leading researchers to call it the new tobacco. Worse still a peptide called gluteo-morphine, in wheat and gluten containing grains, stimulates the opioid centres of our brain just like intoxicating drugs.

APPETITE

The new findings are novel and profound with respect to what controls our moods, emotions and state of mind. In the last decade, researchers have found that the gut (intestines) is a nerve centre so powerful that it is referred to as the second brain. Over 80% of the happiness hormone, serotonin, is secreted in the gut (Refer to *Read more*,

· Makhana, puffed rice or popcorn
· Fresh fruits, fruit salad or chaat
· Dried fruits like raisins, figs, apricots, berries & prunes
· High fibre, low sugar cookies (without hydrogenated fat)
· Flour-less bakery with nut flours
· Grilled & roasted vegetables / paneer / chicken

BEVERAGES
· Herbal and green tea jasmine/chamomile tea
· Regular tea /coffee without sugar
· Cold brew (Refer to *Read more*, page 226)
· Fresh vegetable juices (Refer to *Read more*, page 230) & soups
· Smoothies
· Fruit & vegetable based drinks
· Fresh lime water
· Buttermilk
· Sattoo

page 272). The obvious impact of inflammation in the gut, due to faulty eating and several other environmental and genetic factors could impact our nervous system and psychological health, happiness and mood. What we all know is that our moods affect our food choices. We eat in inappropriate ways and most of the times have poor food choices when hungry, angry, lonely or tired (HALT).

Our appetite regulating hormones; leptin, gherlin, insulin, get unregulated with the inflammation in the gut leading to changes in eating behaviour.

It is not surprising that depression has increased by 18% between 2005-2015, and globally more than 300 million people suffer from depression (World Health Organisation, 2017). Is it not ironic that we have more sources of happiness than ever, yet we are far more unhappy and unhealthy.

GUT-BRAIN CONNECTION
(Refer to *Read more,* page 272)

Current research links the gut to the brain, also called the 'gut-brain axis'. Afflictions in the gut like inflammation, increased permeability (leaky gut), dysbiosis (imbalanced gut flora) thanks to faulty eating, disturb this gut-brain axis, causing it to get unregulated. This leads to a breakdown of our hunger regulating system. These may be responsible for our inability to control our appetite, stick to our diets and regulate body weight. These can cause changes in hunger, appetite and cravings. Often, I hear many patients say we never seem to get full — we can continue snacking even after a full meal, hunger seems like a bottom less inbox!

BREAKDOWN OF OUR INTERNAL CHEMICAL CHECKS AND BALANCES – CONTROLLING APPETITE.

The truth is that we are all born with a fine balance of neurotransmitters and hormones that regulate our appetite. One can never really over feed a baby, if the baby does not want to eat. Not a morsel can be forced. This exemplifies the fact that we are programmed to control our eating but unfortunately, these mechanisms have been destroyed, over years of faulty eating, modifications in the food (refining, processing, and genetically modifying) and agricultural practices. Even animals know when to stop but when we start feeding them our food, they too are hungry all the time. Animals in the wild are never fat but pets in our homes are suffering from serious weight and health issues. This represents in a way what our food is doing to us. It's making us hungrier and unable to regulate our appetite.

> We eat not for health needs rather for taste, comfort and pleasure. A departure from these is unlikely to be a sustainable approach.

SEDUCTIVE ENVIRONMENT AND CLEVER MANIPULATIONS OF OUR MINDS

There is a whole seductive environment, wanting us to eat more and more of the wrong kind of food. It is literally a manipulative hacking of our minds. Billions are spent across industries on food technologists and advertising budgets to make our food addictive. The processes are such that they not only deplete the natural nutrition from the food but they also add artificial elements which harm gut health. Both consciously and subconsciously our food choices are influenced and in many cases governed by advertising. Big companies use clever marketing schemes to lead us to consume more and more, and often portion sizes are manipulated to their advantage.

> You should be able to find comfort in your diet, enjoy it and make it your life partner for optimal health. Else, chances are it will be short-lived.

In addition, food industry also creates temptation by manipulating our senses, also called neuromarketing. We've all experienced this: walked past the food court, seen or smelt something delicious and rushed to order, regardless of its nutritional value. The packaging, display along with advertising and branding lure us. We are tempted by these triggers as the hormone ghrelin is activated in the brain resulting in the desire to eat. The brain is 'attracted' to foods high in sugar and fat rather than healthy foods, when we are hungry. These sensory cues present an on-going challenge to those attempting to eat sensibly.

Another factor is the forbidden foods, which are usually more tempting. Eating sensibly often involves 'giving up' more pleasurable foods. Once we are asked to avoid eating a food we enjoy, we will crave these even more. Hence the behavioural and cognitive response to deprivation often results in creating more temptation.

The guidelines in this book are based on addressing these workplace challenges.

Let's start by redefining diet.

First things first. Diets should not be punitive. A diet does not mean starving, depriving, craving, test of will power or absence of pleasure. Our diet is about eating right. No one, I repeat no one, can eat the same food day in and day out, because we eat for reasons which may, or may not be connected to hunger or our health needs.

Food is an emotive issue. We seek comfort from food. We not only eat when we are hungry but also feed our emotions (HALT) – hungry, angry, lonely and tired. Nowadays, we also eat for entertainment – just like we go to the movies for entertaining ourselves; we go to a restaurant to eat. Eating out is a treat and a pleasurable activity.

Workplace eating, in fact, is not all that different. It is a place where performance appraisals, presentations, targets, socialising and networking alter our eating patterns to a level where we seek comfort in food. Office agendas in conjunction with the domestic ones stretch our bandwidth, adversely affecting our food choices and nutrition. Health too gets bumped to lower levels till that midnight visit to the hospital, which is when introspection and a reality check hits us. Then we look for the ultimate diet plan.

The word diet comes from the Greek word 'Diaita/dieta', which means a 'way of life'. It has very little to do with common perceptions of diets, diet charts and deprivation. Remember that the best diet is the one you never feel you are on, that is, it is completely integrated with your lifestyle and the one you will be able to follow for the rest of your life.

We, therefore, need to redefine and clean up our food, eat simpler, take out the junk, cut back sugars and add plenty of fresh vegetables and fruits (Refer to *Read more,* page 314) and, also, pay attention to our digestion and the gut. This will help restore our normal food regulating systems and support our dietary regimes. In short, you are what you eat – quite literally!

You are what you eat!

Eating right will slowly change you, both in terms of your hunger and preferences. The major change will be in the amount of food you need to feel satiated. Surprisingly, smart eating lowers caloric intake often by less than 50% and increases energy levels. This is completely opposite to the common belief that the more you eat, the more energy you get. The right food keeps craving away and keeps you from choosing unhealthy junk.

The palate too undergoes a change, which might surprise you. Eating right and getting all the nutrients your body needs helps many overcome cravings and correct abnormal eating patterns like compulsive eating, binge eating, night eating, emotional eating, etc. Interestingly, it also changes the love-hate relationship with foods. Often desirable foods like fruits and vegetables which you disliked to begin with, become the central theme of the diet. Many of my patients overcome the desire to eat unhealthy food even when others around them are eating junk. I have seen this happening with most of my clients when they follow my diet plans.

CASE STUDY

An overweight young school-going girl, aged 14 years, was active in sports and used to play for nearly 2 hours every day. She followed a low calorie diet with her only indulgence being a packet of chips a day. On changing her diet and introducing high nutrition foods including raw vegetables, fruits, nuts and seeds, and changing the grains, her addiction to the daily packet of chips simply vanished. This was to the amazement of her family members and caregivers who jokingly said that she was visiting a 'shaman' and not a doctor. This transformation happens to almost all my clients who follow my diet advice. Many sugar addicts who give up sugar, end up finding even natural sweetness in milk too much. Simply put 'you are what you eat!' YOU have the power to change your palate and relationship with food.

THE ULTIMATE DIET PLAN

Let's begin by understanding what the ultimate diet plan is not. It is not standardised. 'An Ideal Diet Plan' does not exist. A manual with all the instructions to suit everybody just does not exist. This vast science when applied to a variety of health needs, tastes and cultural diversity, cannot be over simplified. Each one has to identify the perfect, ultimate and ideal diet plan for themselves, which can withstand their unique challenges including the ones at work like non-availability of certain foods, hygiene, frequent travels and social compulsions. Food requirements can also vary hugely with rapidly growing food sensitivities, personal medical histories and genetic predispositions, needless to add, different ethnic groups and socio-cultural variability.

> It is about acquiring knowledge about what to eat, how to eat, how much to eat and when to eat rather than what not to eat. Then use this information to plan meals and snacks for the day to reach your goals for fitness.

With the number of tools to track calories available today from apps to nutrient information on all packed foods (even some places displaying the calories on menus) we are far from getting fitter, in fact it is quite the opposite. Don't we know about the low calorie, low fat, low carbohydrate, to high fat, high protein, fasting, countless other diets and fitness plans going around? Yet we find these diet plans are short lived and mostly doomed for failure in the long run. What is needed is a sustainable solution. The ultimate diet plan is about busting these myths by setting realistic diet goals while eating for pleasure. It is customised, flexible, sustainable eating that meets our nutritional and health needs. In order to be sustainable, the food has to have variety, visual appeal and be satisfying. It must also be friendly to our ecosystem. Mindful eating has to become a part of your daily routine, and unless you understand your food and your unique needs, there is little chance that you can fight the battle of the bulge. I say food and not simply nutrients. Till now, we have tracked calories, carbohydrates (Refer to *Read more,* page 269), proteins and fats for far too long (almost 2 decades) and remained unsuccessful. The reason is that we eat food and *not nutrients.* Once the right foods are chosen, it is then that calorie counting can be a useful tool to track your intake. Example: if there is a diet of 1200 calories prescribed, it can very well be made up with burger, fries, ice-cream and sugar sweetened colas. This will neither result in weight loss nor well being. Unless we talk in terms of real food and not only nutrients or calories, we cannot be expected to make the right choices. Nutrient calculations are best left to the experts and we need to talk in language of foods understood by the population at large. Our traditional practitioners of health in Ayurveda did not calculate anything. They knew more and ate better!

So the tool box must have information on food to know what to eat, information of when to eat, how to eat and knowledge of your own needs and likes. There is another reality that many are practicing, eating right and engaging in physical activity – and yet are unable to get desired results. Often they get depressed or start following extreme diets or even simply give up. This is dangerous. New science has helped us understand that there are underlying physiological reasons which interfere with weight loss or weight gain. Over the years profound changes in our food supply have impacted us deeply and explain the challenges faced by many.

CHANGES IN QUALITY OF OUR FOOD AND ITS IMPACT ON US

Our bodies and foods have also changed over time. The main reason is the toxic chemical load due to pesticides, herbicides, agricultural practices, genetic modifications, food additives and preservatives. Processing or modification of food and excessive dependence on convenience foods high on fat, sugar, salt and low on nutrients have contributed to altered tolerance to foods. All of this is worsened with overuse of antibiotics, medicines, alcohol, stress and polluted environment. Simply put, the food we are eating and our environment are not what our ancestors ate and were used to. Consequently, our digestive tracts have got insulted. It is not surprising that intolerance to foods and allergies in children, have gone up according to the Centre for Disease Control, United States (CDC) by a whopping 50% between 1997 and 2011 (Jackson KD, Howie LD, Akinbami LJ. Trends in allergic conditions among children: United States, 1997–2011. NCHS data brief, no 121. Hyattsville, MD: National Center for Health

Statistics. 2013). Our food choices must address our individual food sensitivities and allergies.

CASE STUDY

A woman aged thirty, struggling to shed off ten kilograms for many years, wanted to enrol on our online weight management app (www.theweightmonitor. com). She was already clocking in an hour of exercise and following a 1200 calorie diet which is a standard weight loss diet. When asked she said she was eating one burger or sandwich for lunch, one chapatti, lentils and vegetables for dinner and tea with two biscuits or a toast twice a day. Sure she was under 1200 calories but those calories didn't result in weight loss. She turned out to be insulin resistant and sensitive to wheat. As soon as her cereals were replaced with appropriate wheat alternatives she began to drop kilos. This example is not an exception rather it exemplifies majority of people with weight issues. Calorie counting may not work for everyone. Clearly, diets need to be customised and one size doesn't fit all.

DECODING YOUR DIET

In this chapter we learn about foods beyond calories. We decode the IDEAL diet approach in four steps:

1. What to eat and what not to eat?
2. How much to eat?
3. When to eat?
4. How to eat?

FOOD NOT NUTRIENTS

We need to have an understanding of our food, food groups, portion sizes, timings and set goals to arrive at a sustainable diet solution.

We also need to pay attention to how well we digest our food and identify foods that don't agree with us, if any. Since this book is particularly meant for professionals, who already have a lot of information to process and do not want another data point to recall, the information will be crisp, relating it to real food - not calories or nutrients. Generally, when we start monitoring or following diets the first thing we do is to address or track calories. It is believed that eating a certain number of calories a day will keep the extra kilos away. However, calorie counting can be counter-productive, as we seldom stop to think where those calories are coming from. If your target calorie intake is 1200 calories a day, and 500 of those are coming from a samosa and a couple of biscuits downed with tea/ coffee, at the desk while completing the update for the boss, then those 500 calories did more harm than good!

The question is also just the way we count calories, can we track other nutrients like carbohydrates (Refer to *Read more,* page 269), proteins and fats of every single food or meal that we consume? Can we delve into the simple vs complex carbohydrates, saturated vs unsaturated or mono-saturated fats etc.? It is virtually impossible and unwarranted. These are tools for nutritionists and diet professionals. Experience has shown that people find it easier to track food as food groups like vegetables, cereals and lentils rather than keeping a count of the number of calories, carbohydrates, proteins or fat.

Over the last two decades, discussions about food as nutrients like carbohydrates, proteins, fats, calories, vitamins, minerals, fibre and now even as antioxidants, phyto-chemicals, probiotics and prebiotics have become a part of the narrative. Mindfulness about foods, food groups, portions and meal times may be more beneficial than just knowing food as nutrients.

FOOD CHOICES MUST FIT YOUR PREFERENCES

Food choices should not only meet your nutrition and health requirement but these should also be customised and convenient to navigate in different situations. The food choices you make must be as per your food preferences and hunger pattern and must fit in all scenarios including travel, vacation, meetings and conferences. Address the fact that you should be able to sustain your food options whether you are living alone or in a joint family or a paying guest - the possibilities are endless.

WHAT TO EAT AND WHAT NOT TO EAT?

Let's break up the food we eat into food 5 groups such as:
· Vegetables and fruits (protective foods and antioxidants)
· Grains and cereals (carbohydrates)
· Dals and pulses (proteins and carbohydrates)
· Dairy, eggs, fish, chicken or lean meat (proteins)
· Nuts and seeds (fats and proteins)
Sugar and alcohol (Refer to *Read more,* page 244) can be counted in grains and cereals as they metabolize into similar end products.

While planning what to eat, follow the proposition of the half plate rule with food groups (see figure). Half your day's food should comprise of vegetables and some fruits out of which half should ideally be uncooked (salad or vegetables juices or fruits). The remaining half should be divided among the 3 food groups – grains or cereals, pulses and dairy (if consuming), lean meats, eggs, fish, nuts and seeds, commonly referred to as proteins It's easy to remember and simple to follow. For convenience, we can say 50% vegetables and fruits and 30% protein rich foods (pulses, eggs, fish, poultry, meats, nuts, dairy) and 20% cereals. Dairy includes milk, curd, cheese, cottage cheese (paneer) and other dairy products. Since many individuals lose tolerance to dairy and dairy products with age, it is kept as an optional food group. The stress on milk and dairy were strong until its pro-inflammatory effects were noticed by health professionals as also reported by several individuals.

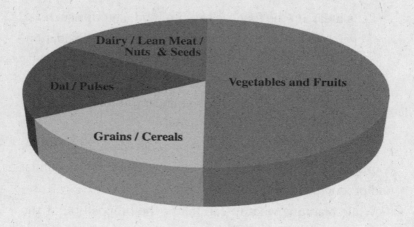

THE ULTIMATE DIET PLAN

In order to make it easy to recall the information on starting your diet we have packed the information on what, how much, when, how to eat in a 5 step approach called the 5Ps

1. Plan
2. Peak hunger time
3. Proteins
4. Pair proteins with vegetables
5. Protective foods

In this chapter we will discuss how you will put the 5 step approach in practice.

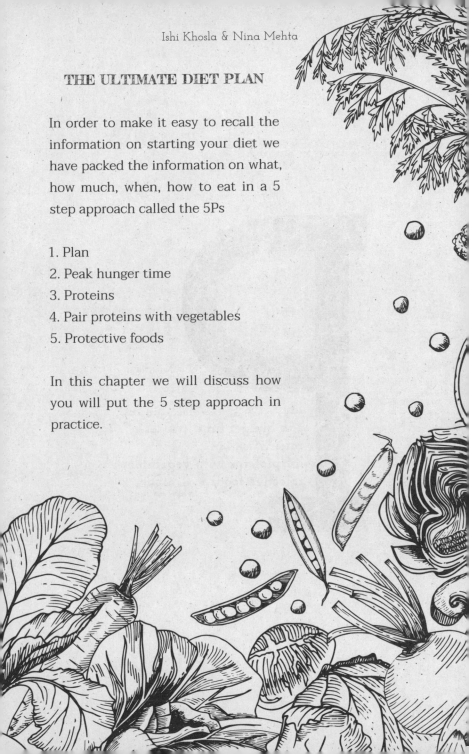

Plan - your day, your choice of cereal, quality & time

Peak hunger time - know your hunger times

Protiens - two meals

Pair proteins with vegetables

Protective foods - dedicate one meal to vegetables and fruits

THE 1ST P
PLAN

PLAN YOUR DAY WITH RESPECT TO FOOD AS FOOD SITUATIONS MAY NOT ALWAYS BE PREDICTABLE.

Engage and get involved in planning and making food decisions. You cannot be passive. It is as important as your business and professional plans.

Just the way you plan your day's meetings, your clothes, plan your food. For example: if you are going to be on the move or if you have a working lunch or social obligation, so on and so forth. This will prevent surprises, situations like 'oh I didn't have a choice'. This will also prevent unwanted gaps, undesirable food intake and binge eating. If you are inclined towards cooking , innovate and explore new ways of cooking with new recipes and cuisines. Plan the ingredients in advance. Plan exercise and supplements.

PLAN THE TIME WHEN YOU WILL HAVE YOUR CEREAL / GRAIN.

Grains or cereals include rice, roti, bread etc. Cereals should not be confused with breakfast cereal. Every cuisine is represented by its staple grains like South Indian cuisine is known by rice, idli, dosa while North Indian cuisine is known by chapattis and paranthas. Italian cuisine is almost synonymous with pasta. China has it's noodles and rice. With the US it's potatoes and breads that you think of first.

Grain or cereal should be eaten ideally before 7 pm and when you are hungriest. These can be paired with vegetables and proteins. Grains or cereals can be included once,twice or thrice a day or none at all, depending on individual requirements.

It is difficult to determine the appropriate amount of grain or cereal for each person. While only one serving of grain or one cereal (example: 1 chapatti or ½ cup rice or a slice of bread refer to table) can be enough for Mr X, ten servings of grains or cereals might not be enough for Mr Y, the difference being their medical history, metabolism and activity.

Typically, in the urban scenario, for people who are not athletic and need to watch their weight, 2–4 servings of grains or cereals are adequate (Refer to *Read more,* page 269) but you do need to understand grain selection.

All grains or cereals are not equal. Grains and cereals are rich in carbohydrate (Refer to *Read more,* page 269) and the nature of carbohydrate can be categorised on the basis of their effects on our blood sugar metabolism. This is called glycemic index.

Glycemic index refers to the ability of a food to raise blood sugar levels in the body. Those foods which release sugars fast are called high glycemic foods or fast carbohydrates while those which release sugars slowly are called low glycemic index foods or slow carbohydrates. Examples of fast carbohydrate foods include cereals like wheat, rice, corn, millets etc. High glycemic index carbohydrates also increase insulin levels and belly fat. Fast carbohydrates can make you feel hungry and tired fast. Slow carbohydrate foods include dals and pulses. Blending flours with pulses, nuts and seeds (flours like almonds, coconut, flax seeds) helps in lowering glycemic index. Such flours have a metabolic advantage for controlling appetite and increasing satiety. Slow carbohydrate foods are preferable in general. As a rule either choose slow carbohydrate or one

> Good fats are essential to health
> Focus on getting healthy fat –
> Nuts, seeds, coconut, avocado
> and cold pressed oils like
> mustard oil, extra virgin olive
> oil, extra virgin coconut oil,
> sesame oil, butter and clarified
> butter (desi ghee).

can combine high and low glycemic carbohydrates. Adding fibre (bran), protein and fats to high glycemic foods helps to lower glycemic index. The practice of adding butter or ghee on roti, rice or bread is based on sound science. For weight management and reduction of belly fat one has to cut back on cereals as these also get converted into sugar. It is advisable to substitute cereals / grains with lentils, pulses, dals (like besan or chana atta), sprouts , or sweet potatoes. Lentils/pulses/dals can be included in the form of chillas or pancakes to replace cereal in one meal. Remember excess of lentils/pulses/dals can disturb your digestion. So have no more than two meals containing dals / pulses. Nut and seed flour like almond flour can be used instead of cereals. Generally speaking grains / cereal at best in one to two meals a day, preferably before sunset.

Alternatively, if you enjoy snacks then use your grain/ cereal allowance as a snack. For example kathi/ roti roll, sandwiches, idlis, dosa, bhel, pizza, burger etc. The other meals may be centred around vegetables/ fruit/ or protein.

SUGAR AND ALCOHOL

(Refer to *Read more*, page 244)

Sugar is the simplest form of carbohydrate. Sugar is also called

Food Groups	Glycemic Index
Cereal products	
White Rice	72
Oats Porridge	49
Quinoa	53
Millets	71
Brown Rice	66
Oat Bran	62
All Bran Cereals	51
Barley	25
Cornflakes	80
Dried Legumes	
Green Gram	48
Black Gram	48
Bengal Gram	47
Chick Peas	33
Lentils	29
Rajmah/ Kidney Beans	27
Soyabeans	15
Vegetables	
Baked Potato	85
Green beans	30
> 50 High GI	
< 50 Low GI	

empty calories as it does not provide any nutrient besides simple carbohydrate. Consumption of excessive sugar in the form of sweets or drinks, tea, coffee, adds calories which can increase insulin levels and belly fat. Excessive sugar can also lead to lower energy, cause fatigue and drowsiness. Sugar has been found to be addictive just like drugs and causes cravings. Besides this it is a major cause of dental caries. Sugar can also disturb the gut flora (candidiasis) leading to leaky gut, inflammation, poor immunity, autoimmune disorders and nutritional deficiencies. While sugar makes food palatable, it is advisable to minimise consumption of simple sugars to no more than 5-7 percent of the total calories (between 4-5 teaspoons a day). Wherever possible substitute simple sugars with unrefined brown sugar, jaggery and honey. Sugar substitutes are widely available but regular consumption can be counter productive. Recent studies associate artificial sweeteners with several diseases including increasing risk to diabetes and obesity. Artificial sweeteners disturb gut flora and can thereby adversely effect our immune system. In other words it may be better to take restricted amounts of natural sugar rather than regularly consume artificial sugar (Refer to *Read more*, page 238).

In general, reduce portions of sweets and avoid regular consumption of sugar sweetened drinks.

Remember sweets when shared becomes sweeter!

Alcohol: The dose makes the poison. While moderate alcohol which is equivalent to 2 small drinks can provide benefits, the third can be toxic. The damage is not only to the liver where it is detoxified but also to the gut lining. Keep to the rule of moderation. Recent studies demonstrate that there is no safe level of alcohol intake. (Refer to *Read more*, page 244)

Grain sensitivity: One of the major paradigm shifts in food is a moving away from grains like wheat. Wheat is among the most traditional, respected and recommended part of our diet.

This is because of the incredible changes in agricultural practices. Biotechnologists are modifying seeds to increase yield, and developing pesticides resistant crops. There is a dramatic increase in the use of pesticides and other chemical fertilizers in the last 50 years. Modifications in seeds have led to chromosomal changes which have perhaps become foreign to our bodies evoking immune reactions, more severely in genetically predisposed and younger people. Milk and dairy too have undergone similar changes in their proteins making them inflammatory in nature.

In-fact, 50% of those intolerant to wheat are estimated to be dairy intolerant.

ALTERNATIVES TO WHEAT

Besides rice some of the lesser known and forgotten grains are millets which include bajra, jowar, ragi, quinoa (south American grain)and teff, (south African staple cereal). India is a reservoir of diverse grain, and many consume them during the fasting period of (navratras) for 9 days twice a year. These grains are better tolerated, and easier to digest. Lentils or chickpea flours and nut flours can double up as cereals.

Individual difference in response to each of the cereals may be there. To understand your body's specific needs a food sensitivity test (IgG) is advisable.

GRAIN FREE APPROACH
(Refer to *Read more,* page 269)

Many people are following extremely low carbohydrates diets like Keto, Paleo, Atkins etc. which are mostly devoid of grains / cereals. A word of caution, when cutting back on your grain or cereal intake it is advisable to substitute these with healthier alternatives. For example: vegetables, dals, sprouts, fruit, nuts and seeds.

Vegetables can be taken as cooked vegetables, vegetable

Grains/Cereals at work: Meal in a bowl

Curd, roasted grains (namkeen), chopped relish of onions, tomatoes, green coriander, chillies.

Rice/ quinoa/ boiled grain with lentils and onion relish.

Wraps (regular rice roti / quinoa roti wraps/ chilla wraps/ dosa wraps).

Roti with twists: made with alternate flours, stuffed roti's.

Rice based: dosa, idli, poha, puttoo, appam, padthai, rice noodles, moong bean noodles, brown rice, black rice, red rice, quinoa, millets.

Non cereal alternatives: cauliflower rice, radish grated.

---

juices (Refer to *Read more,* page 230) or salad. Be careful of excess proteins in the form of lentils, eggs, chicken, fish or meat. A lot of people think that they can do away completely with cereals but it is really not necessary to do so. In case you must it is best done under professional guidance.

Most people are accustomed to their grains or cereals and feel so comforted by these that they can't do without their staples, which are their comfort foods too. Hence they lapse back to old eating habits.

PLAN EXERCISE

Eating before exercise is counter productive specially if you are trying to lose weight. A high carbohydrate snack like a fruit, lemon water with salt and coconut water are ideal. Post exercise proteins combined with carbohydrates are best. A glass of vegetables juice will be great. Ideally a gap of at least 2 hours between your meal and exercise is advisable. For high intensity exercise guidelines need to be modified.

PLAN WHEN YOU WILL HAVE YOUR SUPPLEMENTS

Taking super foods and supplements in the morning ensures better regularity. Keep your post dinner supplements on your bedside table. For travel or at work keep them in your bag/desk. Special pill boxes work well.

PLAN YOUR GOAL POSTS

BMI, weight, waist size and other health goals.
Body mass index (BMI)
Measure of degree of obesity

BMI= Weight (kg)/ht (m2)

Ideal BMI < 23.0 kg /m2

Your ideal weight

For men, 48kg for the first 5 feet + 2.7 kg per inch

For women, 45kg for the first 5 feet + 2.5kg per inch

Waist circumference (WC) (measured around abdomen)

Women ≤ 80 cms (<31.5 inches)

Men   ≤ 90 cms (<35.5 inches)

Calculate your caloric requirement.

· Weight in pounds x 15 for a normal lifestyle.

· Weight in pounds x 13 for a sedentary lifestyle.

Remember you first need to know what to eat and then use this as a guiding tool. Quality of calories is most important

PRACTICE THE PRINCIPLES OF HEALTHY EATING

Principles of healthy eating are common sense rules which allow you to practice healthy eating in a sustainable manner. Always keep these in mind when you plan: Moderation, balance and variety.

MODERATION

No food is good or bad; what matters is the amount you take. When you proclaim foods 'off limits', you are setting up a rule just waiting to be broken. Portion control is key to healthy eating. A small portion of dessert rather than the entire helping will be a good idea and is unlikely to conflict with your goals, unless you are intolerant to it.

BALANCE

There may be days when moderation or portion control fails. You go through the entire dessert and feel terribly guilty. Don't let lapses become collapses. The principle of balance helps you undo the damage and lighten the next meal to compensate for the previous one, and this will ensure that you do not mess up your goals. Balance may also be achieved by engaging in physical activity, by walking that extra mile. Balance can be anticipatory or retrospective. Anticipatory balance refers to the following if you are likely to overeat later in the day, under-eat or lighten your meal before that. Retrospective balance implies damage control after eating more than you should have. If you like to snack all day, then eat less at meal times, have more vegetables, soup, salad, fruits or yoghurt. Balance can be adopted as a lifelong habit. Having alternate days of detox diet with vegetables (soups/ salads/ steamed/ vegetables/ vegetable juices/ sprouts) along with some fruits is a great way to keep your diet excesses in check and from affecting you negatively. If not alternate days, then maybe at least the days after you've over-eaten or eaten badly, a detox day will be helpful. This is also called alternate day fasting. In fact fasting is both a traditional and scientific approach to balance out excesses through the week. The popularity of the intermittent fasting (Refer to *Read more*, page 273) diet is growing. This technique which limits the number of hours of eating has found its way into many people's lives. For example if you have eaten late at night the next day you will be better off either doing a detox diet or starting to eat later in the day, say, lunch time.

VARIETY

Variety is indeed the spice of life. How many different foods do you eat every day: ten-fifteen? Would it surprise you that one of Japan's dietary guidelines suggested eating thirty different foods each day? Variety ensures that your body gets all the nutrients it needs. Make sure that you include foods from all the food groups, and maintain variety within food groups. For example, an apple is rich in vitamin E and poor in vitamin C while an orange is rich in vitamin C and poor in vitamin E. Eating both ensures that you get enough of both the nutrients. Eating a variety of foods prevents food sensitivities. For instance, within the 'grains/cereal' food group, eating a variety of grains is better than subsisting only on a single grain.

THE 2ND P
PEAK HUNGER TIME

Most of us have a specific time when we are hungriest. Some people are hungry at breakfast, some at lunch and most in the evening. Whatever be it understand your body clock and try to eat most of your food during those hours – at least your grain/ cereal. According to observational studies the time between 5-7 coincides with maximum ordering in of snacks at work. It is prudent to plan your cereal intake at this time so that you avoid the temptation of eating unhealthy junk food (remember grains/ cereals are best eaten before 7 pm). If you are not hungry in the morning, lunch may be your first meal. If you like you can maintain a food diary to know your peak hunger time. Resist eating late at night even if you are hungry.

Data collected from about 10000 clients at my centre suggests that peak hunger time is either around lunchtime or between 5 pm and 7 pm. Since the peak hunger time for working people is between 5pm and 7 pm, it is advisable to eat a meal at this time and eat a lighter meal or healthy snack later. Aim to eat cereals/ grains, sandwiches, rotis, idlis etc. and then go home and have vegetables, soups, salad, fruits or some protein-rich food. Have grains at the time your hunger peaks.

You may also try and eat your last meal of the day by 8 pm. If later than 8 pm then either skip the grain and have fruits, nuts, seeds, soup, or milk. Even then if you have eaten the grain, all is not lost. Go for a walk or balance the next day by eating more fruits, vegetables like a detox diet.

THE 3ʳᵈ P
PROTEIN

Aim to include two protein rich meals in a day. These could be in the form of pulses, dals, nuts, dairy, eggs, lean meat, chicken and fish.

Eating a couple of servings of dals and pulses a day is adequate as excess could lead to gastric distress and bloating. |Lentil pancakes (chillas) should also be counted as proteins. There is a tendency towards too much protein among the youth. Taking protein supplements (read more protein equal to muscle) has become the norm for those going to gyms. This is not warranted unless you are engaged in high levels of sporting activity. If you engage in intensive physical exercise like endurance exercise or heavy weight training protien intake would need to increase. In most individuals doing moderate exercise, dietary protein should be enough to meet requirements. Excess animal protein should also be avoided.

MAKING GRAINS, LENTILS AND PULSES EASY TO DIGEST.

Soak grains or cereals, pulses (even nuts like almonds) before consuming as far as possible to prevent bloating and improve absorption of nutrients and digestion. Soaking helps in removal of lectins (Refer to *Read more,* page 284) which can irritate the digestive tract.

Protein is an essential nutrient which helps to build our body to ensure normal body functions. Proteins are a source of essential amino acids which repair our cells including gut lining. While the right amount of protein is important excess protein is harmful.

For the general population 0.75 gms per day per kg body weight is adequate. With certain conditions or increase in exercise this needs to be stepped up to 1gm per kg body weight. *Note this is per kg and not per pound of body weight.* Most protein supplements are soya, whey (dairy) based which can be detrimental for many people with food sensitivities and digestive issues

THE 4ᵀᴴ P
PAIR THE PROTEIN WITH VEGETABLES

Proteins are acidic in nature and are best taken with an alkaline food like vegetables or fruits. Ensuring that you combine protein with salads, vegetable juices, cooked vegetables or fruits makes them easier to digest and also provide more fibre to aid digestion.

PROTEIN IDEAS

Plant protein: Lentil pancakes (chilla), moong idli, moong daal, laddu, sprouts, chana chaat, matra, chana tikki, dhokla, khandvi, falafel, sundal, vegetable pakora, vada, daal dosa, sautéed peas and mushrooms

Animal protein: Eggs, chicken kebabs, chicken grilled, chicken stir-fry, fish steamed, fish grilled, fish cutlets, fish fried, lamb kebabs, lamb stew

---

THE 5ᵀᴴ P
PROTECTIVE FOODS

VEGETABLES AND FRUITS

So important is this group in the current lifestyle that one must try to dedicate one meal to this group. Vegetables can be cooked, grilled, made into a soup or salad or had as a vegetable juice.

> Include functional and anti-inflammatory foods like Aloevera, Amla (Indian gooseberry), Basil (Tulsi), Lemon, Honey, Turmeric etc. in the morning.

Not only do vegetables and fruits fortify our health, they also lay the foundation of good eating. Loaded with antioxidants, phyto-chemicals, vitamins, minerals and fiber, this low calorie high nutrient group is one of the most valuable elements in our current lifestyles. This group has been called protective foods simply because they have phyto nutrients (plant nutrients) which help fight diseases. Those which have exceptionally high levels of phyto nutrients are also popularly called super foods.

No healthy meal can be complete without vegetables – salads, soups or cooked vegetables. You can eat plenty of raw vegetables without worrying about calories. They can almost be treated as free foods. They help in repairing our cells and detoxifying our bodies. Potatoes, sweet potatoes, and other starches need to be watched as they are high on carbohydrates which turn into sugars. They can in fact replace grains and cereals.

Vegetables and fruits are central to good health and make sure you include fruits and also a good mix of both raw and cooked vegetables to make the most of their benefits.

Smart food checklist

AIM TO EAT DAILY

1 carrot, 1 cucumber, 1 tomato /
1 beetroot, 1 seasonal saag (green leafy vegetables), 1 lemon/ amla, 1 seasonal fruit, handful of nuts, seeds, sprouts or chana.

If you suffer from digestive issues and find it difficult to digest raw vegetables, it is better to steam or cook them. Try to replace raw vegetables with some fruit instead until you fix your system. Usually these digestive issues can be traced to food sensitivities (dairy, wheat etc.). You must address this as a sign and get the necessary blood test for food intolerances (Refer to *Read more,* page 260).

FRUITS AND FRUIT JUICES
(Refer to *Read more,* page 314)

While fruits are loaded with antioxidants and micro-nutrients, they are also a source of sugar (fructose), so modest intake of fruit (1-3 serving) is adequate. Avoid fruit juices as they are concentrated sources of sugar and spike our blood sugar leading to imbalance of insulin levels resulting in sugar cravings, low blood sugars, belly fat, fatty liver and high uric acid.

WHEN TO EAT FRUITS

The issue on when to eat fruits has been a subject of much discussion. While modern science does not address this traditional systems of medicine like Ayurveda have clear guidelines. According to this system fruits are best taken on an empty stomach. Further fruits are best taken in the morning and their benefits are believed to be depleted if taken later in the day. Proponents of this theory state that fruits should never be eaten with or immediately following anything. They believe that fruits if not eaten correctly can ferment or putrefy causing formation of acid waste which is counter productive. A toxic acid system can be recognised by bloating, flatulence, weight gain, and premature ageing, anxiety and skin changes.

In other words, it's not recommended to eat fruits for dessert as they start fermenting in the stomach while waiting for their turn to be assimilated. It is also stated that those who have a strong digestive system may eat fruits any time of the day.

While no scientific research can back these claims clinical experience supports the merits, specially among persons who have dysbiosis (imbalanced gut flora like candidiasis) or digestive disorders. This means they are best in the morning or 3-4 hours after a meal.

Meanwhile the message is to treat fruits as an invaluable part of the diet. They are easy to digest, have high water content, are loaded with valuable disease fighting elements like enzymes, fibre, prebiotics, vitamins, minerals, antioxidants, are alkaline in nature and of course delicious to taste. Excessive fruit intake should be guarded against specially if you are overweight, diabetic or have a digestive disorder. This means they are best in the morning or 3-4 hours after a meal.

Whole fruits are preferable to fresh fruit juices. If you feel better eating fruits at a particular time of the day then ensure you respect your body's preference. There may also be individual intolerance for certain fruits. Listening to your body is important. Remember you are unique.

If you can adopt the wisdom of eating fruits the right way you surely stand to benefit from these wonderful gifts of nature. Aim to have at least one to two servings of seasonal

---

PROTECTIVE FOODS CAN ALSO BE CALLED PRANA (LIFE) OR PHYTO (PLANT) FOODS. DEDICATE ONE MEAL TO THIS GROUP.

Salads

Vegetables juices

Grilled / tandoori/ steamed vegetables

Stir fried vegetables

Vegetable cutlets

Cauliflower rice

Fresh fruit salad

Fruit chaat

Sprouts

Hot / cold soup

fruits on a daily basis, preferably at breakfast or as a snack.

SUPER FOODS

Food has been recognised as a medicine for thousands of years. Good food is medicine and can help delay, prevent and at times treat diseases. Wrong food can make us unwell and sick. Several dietary constituents and nutrients are comprehensively documented with their protective roles

---

CEREAL VS VEGETABLES AND FRUITS

Contrary to what our forefathers said, grains and cereals are side dishes, not fillers anymore. In the older generation the requirement of grains which are energy giving foods was much higher due to their active lifestyles and higher energy expenditure. However, that is not the case now, unless someone is involved in manual physical work or active sports. As a matter of fact, the balance has to shift in favour of protective foods, rich in phyto-nutrients, found in vegetables and fruits to maintain good health and fight the unprecedented levels of toxins in our environment, be it air pollutants, heavy metals, pesticide-laden water or radiation.

---

in health and diseases. The kitchen is indeed the best pharmacy. One needs to be knowledgeable about these foods and their benefits. Include aloevera, amla, turmeric, ginger, basil, spirulina, curry leaves, moringa, seaweeds, berries, spice waters, dry fruits, nut and seeds in your diet.

Spice water with cumin, fennel, carom seeds, ginger.

HOW MUCH TO EAT?

CALORIES:
It is important to remember that counting calories is useful only if the composition of the diet is correct. Generally the servings below is a reasonable guide. Individual requirements can vary hugely.

GRAINS/CEREALS: On an average a moderately active person may consume 5–8 serving of grain/

What counts as a serving of GRAINS / CEREALS

Bread 1 (medium) slice
Bagel ¼ (large)
Bhatura ½
Biscuits 2–3
Boiled corn ½ cup
Bread roll 1 (medium)
Corn on the cob (bhutta) ½ (medium)
Chapatti 1 (medium)
Crackers 6
Dry flour 3 tbsp
French fries 1 cup/10 pieces
Hamburger/hot dog bun (½ a bun)
Idli 1 (large)
Kulcha 1 (medium)
Muesli/granola ¼ cup/3 tbsp
Naan (8x2 inches) 1/3
Noodles (cooked) ½ cup
Pasta (cooked) ½ cup
Pita bread ½ (medium)
Pizza (thin crust) 2 (medium) slices

Plain dosa 1 (medium) length of a table knife

Poha/upma (cooked) ½ cup

Popcorn 3 cups

Porridge (cooked) ½ cup

Potato* 1 (medium)

Potato chips 1/ 3 cup

Puffed cereal 1½ cups

Rice (murmura)

Rice (cooked) ½ cup

Roasted rice flakes (chirwa) 1/ 3 cup/3-4 tbsp

Sandwich 1 triangle/rectangle

* In nutrition science, potatoes and starchy vegetables like colocasia (arbi), sweet potatoes and yam are not a part of the 'fruit' or 'vegetable' groups and are included under 'grains/cereals', owing to their high carbohydrate content.

cereal in a day. But those trying to lose weight should reduce the portion.

PROTIENS (LEGUMES & DAIRY, EGGS, MEAT, FISH: Include at least 2–3 servings of pulses/ legumes/ lentils, beans, if you are a vegetarian. However, if you consume animal protein as dairy, eggs, meat, fish, these may: be only 0–2 servings each day depending on your consumption of these. Try and include a serving of sprouts (Refer to *Read more*, page 266) on most days as they are little nutrient factories which also contain beneficial enzymes.

VEGETABLES: Vegetable servings can be at least 4–6 servings a day. 50% of these should be eaten raw. One serving is about half cup of most vegetables and one cup of green leafy vegetables.

FRUITS: Try and include at-least 1–2 seasonal fruits a day.

NUTS AND SEEDS: A fistful or 30–50 gms a day is a reasonably healthy portion.

Healthy fats include coconut, avocado and cold pressed oils like mustard, sesame, virgin coconut, extra virgin olive oil, butter and desi ghee (clarified butter). Reused oils, hydrogenated margarines and vanaspati must be avoided as they are hidden sources of harmful trans-fats. Trans-fats are also found in most commercially available fried foods, biscuits, bakery, rusks, cakes etc.

BEGIN YOUR JOURNEY TO WELLNESS

THE FLUID FACTOR

Let's first understand what fluids include. Fluids really include water, juices, beverages, soups, tea, coffee (Refer to *Read more*, page 226), milk and all other beverages except alcohol (Refer to *Read more*, page 244). Even though tea and coffee are diuretics and cause loss of water from the body, for calculations, they contribute to our fluid intake. In our discussion, we will first discuss water followed by other caffeinated drinks.

We all know that about 60–70% of our body is water. The connection between this fact and how much fluid is to be consumed is hardly ever made. Most of us drink water only when thirsty. This can be a huge mistake as thirst is not a reliable indicator of how much water we need. Often we mistake thirst for hunger. Taking enough water can keep us away from over eating. Adequate water can also help improve concentration.

Water and fluids are critically important in the detoxification process of our bodies. Unfortunately, there is no 'dry cleaning' and we need to get rid of the toxic waste through urine and sweat. Water is also critical to the body for digestion, absorption, transport of nutrients, elimination and regulation of body temperature. Insufficient water intake can significantly decrease work performance, cause indigestion, constipation, hyper-acidity, risk to renal (kidney) stones or urinary tract infections. These can further impact our skin, hair and appetite. In fact, adequate water intake promotes metabolism and circulation. It impacts our enzymes and health of our gut microbiome (the delicate balance between good and bad bacteria in the gut). Toxins such as pollutants, chemicals, food additives and many carcinogens are flushed out of the body by adequate water intake. It is obvious that inadequate water intake will prevent detoxification. It will also

Drinking adequate water could mean different amounts for different individuals in different places, situations and physical activity. However, a basic minimum of 6–8 glasses is needed for smooth functioning of our body and vital organs. While it comes naturally to some, others may need to make a special effort and be a little more aware of their water intake. Just by increasing a few glasses daily, you can overcome many health conditions, especially common complaints of indigestion. Drinking water the right way can also help you stay fit and keep hunger away.

Those who drink less because of not feeling thirsty or feeling less thirsty compared to others, may experience bloating after drinking water. For some this may be a sign of some digestive discomfort linked to a food intolerance. Once the underlying cause of digestive discomfort is addressed, there may be an increase in thirst and water intake.

Those who shy away from water for its lack of taste, can use infused water, herbal teas, lemon or ginger or turmeric or spice water, water stored in coloured bottles or dispensed in kettles with tea lights. These are some of the ways to boost not only the fluid factor but also a functional and anti-inflammatory quotient to it.

slow down metabolism, subsequently increase body weight. To ensure good hydration it is recommended that drinking water an hour before meals will ensure optimum intake of water. After waking up in the morning, take 1–2 cups of water, 1–2 cups an hour before lunch and before dinner respectively. However, avoid consuming large quantities of water with meals. A few sips are okay. Also, it is advisable to avoid pairing your meals with sugar sweetened soda on a routine basis as you will unnecessarily add a huge sugar load (7–8 teaspoons) and also make your body acidic.

Individual needs definitely vary according to the body type, body weight, weather and activity. Try to consume good quality and quantity of water as far as possible. It should be alkaline and microbially pure with plenty of minerals. Water stored in silver and copper vessels is a good idea. Avoid water stored in plastics.

Your brain is 75% water. When we become dehydrated,our brain actually shrinks,which can effect our functionality. According to research children who are mildly dehydrated perform poorly at school and benefit from drinking water which improves their cognitive performance. Hydration status effects mood and low fluid intake increases sleepiness, fatigue, vigour, alertness and increase confusion. Water absorption begins very rapidly from mouth to blood streams peaking in around 20 minutes. To know if you are dehydrated watch the colour of your urine. Ideally it should be as light as possible. Dark urine indicates the need to drink more. The symptoms of dehydration include lethargy, fatigue, headaches, stomach-ache, confusion and dry lips.

SOME TIPS TO ENSURE YOU DRINK RIGHT

1. Try to drink water slowly.

2. Take sips with meals.

3. Avoid drinking too much right before or during meals.

4. Avoid drinking cold/ chilled water with meals.

5. Try to consume up-to half a litre in between meals, ideally 1 hour after eating.

6. Start your day with water at room temperature or lukewarm water.

7. Hot water/ liquids are more filling than cold.

8. Store drinking water in earthen pots, copper or silver vessels to enhance its value.

9. Ensure you drink an extra glass of water with each cup of tea, coffee and alcoholic drink to compensate for the diuretic effect of these beverages.

10. Dark coloured urine indicates need to drink more.

HEALTHY FLUIDS

Pure water (cool or hot) alkaline if possible

Infused waters (fruit/ vegetables/leaves like mint/celery / spices)

Kahawa

Green / white tea (green tea with saffron, matcha tea) (Refer to *Read more,* page 223)

Diluted fruit juices with still or sparkling water / soda

Butter milk (lassi/chaanch)

Coconut water (could be with chia / basil seeds)

Iced tea

Black tea with lemon, with or without honey

Coffee with cardamom

Vegetables juices and smoothies

Coconut milk flavoured with fruit juice

Kokum juice (Refer to *Read more,* page 228)

Satto

TEA AND COFFEE
(Refer to *Read more*, page 220)

No office works without tea or coffee. It is the very nature of these drinks (i.e. the caffeine kick) which makes them so important, and hence the risks. For many, the added sugar and milk poses an additional risk. Worse still, it is the partnership of that cup of tea/ coffee with biscuits/ cookies/ rusks. A single cup of tea with biscuits and a teaspoon of sugar can take up the entire day's sugar allowance. Limit tea or coffee intake to no more than 2-3 cups a day. Excess can be irritating to the stomach / gut lining due to tannic acid and caffeine content. This can also increase inflammation, gastritis and increase the risk of stomach cancer. According to Dr Hiromi Shinya, a leading Japanese gastroenterologist, those patients of his who drank excessive tea and coffee had thinning and atrophic changes of the gastic lining. Being diuretics, tea and coffee increase water loss. This is accompanied by loss of valuable magnesium (Refer to *Read more,* page 286) and other electrolytes. Magnesium deficiency is highly under recognised and under diagnosed. Magnesium is important in controlling 300 functions in the body. Common deficiency symptoms includes sleep disturbances, migraines, water retentions, cramps, anxiety and constipation. Drinking six or more cups of coffee a day can be harmful and increase the risk of heart ailment by up to 22 percent, revealed in a study published in *The American Journal of Clinical Nutrition.* (Refer to *Read more,* page 286).

Try to drink plain water instead of tea or coffee. Many drink to curb appetite, to boost energy, concentration and exercise performance. Whatever be the reason, try to maintain no more than 2-3 cups of tea/ coffee. Green tea in excess can also cause gastritis or irritation to the gut.

CHEWING WELL

Most of the traditional practitioners of health and our grandparents too emphasised the practice of at least 15-32 times chewing well. The most important reason for chewing food well is to allow time for the food to be mixed well with enzyme rich saliva and get broken down for better absorption. However, if we don't chew well, larger food particles enter our gut causing leaky gut. The intestinal wall of a person can absorb substances up-to 15 microns (0.15 mm) in size. Anything bigger is secreted or leaks into the gut. By chewing well you ensure better particle size.

Secondly it prevents you from overeating as it simply takes longer to finish the meal and the brain takes approximately 20 minutes to give the signal for fullness. By eating slowly you get that time to experience fullness and hunger is surpassed adequately and you are satisfied with lesser food.

Though for busy working people this may sound daunting but nonetheless this principle truly works. Young children must be taught to eat slowly and chew well for this habit to develop. It is never too late! Remember, it takes 21 days of practice to develop any new habit.

FOOD SHARING AND EATING IN COMPANY

Often my patients mention that over-eating happens when they are sitting together with colleagues or friends at work. While this is a positive environment overeating needs to be watched. One can lose track of how much one is eating when one tastes others' food or in conversation. The best way to be mindful is to start tracking your intake through a food diary. Always stop eating when you are just pleasantly full and before you are completely full.

FORGETTING TO EAT

During my experience as a counsellor I notice two distinct types of eating behaviour;

1. Those who eat mindlessly and need to graze all the time to concentrate.

2. Those who can eat only after they are done with their work. These people often forget eating.

Know who you are. Whatever you prefer ensure that you do not overeat while grazing. If you are the one who forgets to eat ensure you avoid having long gaps and binge later. Take plenty of water and fluids to keep yourself going. Productivity can drop with dehydration.

FOOD DIARY
(Refer to *Read more*, page 289)

The most powerful tool to keep you on track is the food

diary or your food log. Most of us underestimate what we eat and overestimate our exercise. Keeping a food diary allows you to record everything you eat and drink. You can see the reality of what you eat and even auto correct. Adding details of the eating experience makes it even more meaningful as what you eat is often influenced by what's going on inside and around you. You can record it online which may be more convenient than pen and paper.

SNACKS VS. MEALS

Some people just don't want snacks and they are happy with three meals. Some studies suggests it is better to eat small frequent meals with snacks. However, nothing is etched in stone and follow what you prefer.

EAT LESS EAT BETTER

Eating better quality and less food can be helpful in the long run. In-fact fasting regularly has been a tool to achieve good health and longevity (Refer to *Read more*, page 277).

CASE STUDY

One of my clients, a shop-owner who lost 49 kgs in a year, could not eat dinner in his shop and had to eat it at home which was at 9 pm at the earliest. So he found a way by eating a bowl of grilled vegetables and soups for dinner. This meant two chillas (lentil pancakes) in the morning, salad and nuts in the afternoon while attending to customers and then dinner at 9PM was mainly vegetables.. He continues to maintain this even after 6 years.

NAVIGATING TRAVEL, MEETINGS AND CONFERENCES

These can really throw you off your diet and exercise regimens. Yet they are an integral part of working life. Since they cannot be and need not be wished away smart eating strategies can ensure that no damage is done to your diet. Food choices, timings and exercise schedules can change. Usually dinners are heavy and late. Use the 5Ps to navigate these situations.

1. Plan your day and reserve eating most of your food for social and professional engagements, conferences and meetings. Eating fruits for breakfast and vegetables, salad and soups for lunch and proteins for dinner. If you are hungry you can pair fruits at breakfast with nuts, eggs or sprouts. Soup can provide excellent satiety and can see you through with very few calories. Needless to say these should be without noodles, pasta, croûtons and wontons.

2. Avoid heavy dinners. If unavoidable, then skip the grains/cereals and sweets.

3. Balance out your diet the next day.

4. Eat healthy during meetings and avoid unnecessary snacking on biscuits, bakery products and oily carbohydrate-rich snacks. Choose nuts and fruits if possible.

5. Keep lunch light as far as possible. Soups and salads with cooked vegetables, boiled beans, sprouts, hummus, are great options.

6. Watch your alcohol intake. In-case you wish to take alcohol then cut out the carbohydrates in the form of grains and desserts. For convenience treat one cereal as one alcoholic drink.

7. When travelling (Refer to *Read more*, page 306), ensure you carry healthy snacks like nuts, fruits, energy bars or balls (laddus) made with dry fruits, nuts and seeds. Those are easy options so you do not need to snack on unhealthy foods on the way.

8. Try and stick to your exercise regimen as far as possible.

Meeting Snacks

Toasted nuts

Dried fruits

Fresh fruits

Roasted chick peas

Cracker and dip

Dhokla

Idli (mini)

NAVIGATING YOUR WAY THROUGH BUFFETS

· If you have to eat a buffet, take a look at all the food that is there, step back and then decide what really tempts you. Take one helping and remember your portions and the half-plate rule.

· Before going to a restaurant, drink (one hour before) two glasses of water or vegetables juice or eat some fruit to curb your appetite.

· Start your meals with appetizers like clear soups and salads and vegetables. When unsure about hygiene, avoid uncooked salads and raw preparations and stick with cooked vegetables.

· Choose a protein of your choice which could mean meats, fish, pulses, lentils or cheese.

· Processed meats like ham, salamis, sausages and bacon should not be taken on a regular basis. Occasionally these are okay. However if you suffer from digestive issue, these are best avoided.

· Cereals can be portioned as per grain / cereal allowance for the day. Remember if you eat a dessert you are likely to exceed your grain/ cereal allowance.

· Avoid sugar, sweetened beverages, mock-tails and cocktails.

WHILE ORDERING A-LA CARTE

If you like variety and want to try different things, order a variety of starters (preferably non-fried), rather than a heavy main course. Skip the bread basket. While waiting ask for olives or vegetable sticks.

FOOD SENSITIVITY (READ MORE ON FOOD SENSITIVITY AND LEAKY GUT)

(Refer to *Read more,* page 244)

• When you are eating right by the book and ticking all the boxes when it comes to the weight watching checklist, yet issues of weight and related conditions are bothering you, it is time to look deeper for answers. That is, look into the matters of the gut.

• Be it your weight, waist, health conditions, energy, sleep deprivation, mood swings, skin or hair issues — sometimes conventional wisdom does not point you to the underlying cause. The truth is it may have everything to do with the food you eat everyday.

• Disturbance in the gut microbiome is called dysbiosis. This leads to breakdown of regulatory mechanism of hunger and appetite. If the food that you eat causes an immune reaction and disturbs your intestinal flora it causes an impairment of the intestinal barrier also called increased permeability/ hyper permeability or leaky gut syndrome. The gut is home for not only digestion, absorption and elimination but also plays the important role of a barrier – it regulates immune and neurological functions and helps to maintain hormone balance. Any impairment in the gut – as in the leaky gut – can increase inflammation and weaken the entire body. In other words it's not only what you eat but what you digest.

• Research shows the most common triggers in food which can cause food sensitivities include gluten, wheat, dairy and dairy products. These reactions are measured by antibodies called IgG. The IgG positive foods indicate that your immune system responds adversely to these foods. In case you feel better by eliminating these inflammatory grains and dairy foods, seek professional help to accurately diagnose your food sensitivities.

Travel tips to those on selected grain diet :(Food Sensitivity) Prefer Indian , South Indian Grilled , Mediterranean , Japenese, Thai , Korean cuisines. Keep faithful to the grain selection Eat two meals with proteins. Ensure one meal is a salad or fruit. If you excess on food keep to soup and salad in the next. Treat alcohol as cereal . In case you do drink avoid cereal that day. Alcohol restriction to two or two wines .Avoid beers Be careful of soya sauce, tofu in soups, stir fries & Chinese food. Avoid corn based Mexican food Check ingredients of gluten free food (no oats / corn / soya) Walk as much as possible and enjoy.

If you suffer from one or more of the mentioned signs and symptoms you may be suffering from food sensitivity issues. It is important to understand that you may have had these foods all your life but can develop adverse responses to a particular food any time of your life. Stress, physical or mental trauma, injuries, surgeries, or illness or hormonal therapies changes through puberty, pregnancy, post pregnancy, pre-menopause or menopause can trigger a leaky gut leading to food sensitivities.

Common signs & symptoms of food sensitivities include:

· Difficulty in losing weight, increased belly fat and bloating.

· Unexplained weight loss

· Growth retardation and delayed puberty

· Chronic anxiety or depression or irritability

· Brain fog, ADHD, ADD and forgetfulness

· Pain in the joints

· Mouth ulcers and tooth discolouration

     · Pale sores inside the mouth

     · Pale, foul-smelling stool

· Tingling and numbness in the legs

· Chronic fatigue

· Recurring abdominal bloating and pain

· Hyper-acidity reflux or gastric ulcers or nausea or vomiting

· Irritable Bowel Syndrome, constipation, ulcerative colitis or Chron's disease.

· Liver disease

· Polycystic ovaries, infertility and recurrent miscarriages

· Bone density issues from Osteopenia to Osteoporosis

· Skin rashes, eczema, psoriasis, hair fall (alopecia)

· Vitiligo, dry skin, dry eyes

· Autoimmune diseases (thyroid, Rheumatoid arthritis, multiple selerosis, Lupus etc.)

According to Dr Tom O Bryan a functional Medicine expert about one third of the population may be suffering from wheat intolerance. Sensitivity to wheat has increased five folds since 1974 (ANN Med. 2010) and signs and symptoms can be non-specific and 90% cases remain undiagnosed the average time from symptoms to diagnoses is 10 years. According to Dr. Alessio Fasano (Director of Pediatric Gastroenterology General Hospital for Children, Boston), almost 300 health conditions are linked to wheat intolerance.

In case you test positive to gluten, some of the other grains which need to be watched include:
· Wheat and its derivatives
– Refined flour (maida), semolina (suji or rava or couscous) broken wheat porridge (dalia)
· Barley
· Rye
· Oats
· Corn
· Soya
About 50% of people who are sensitive to gluten are sensitive to dairy.

'THE ROAD TO GOOD HEALTH IS PAVED WITH GOOD INTESTINES'
SHERRY ROGERS

EMOTIONAL EATING

We eat when we are hungry. We eat when we are angry but not necessarily hungry. At times we eat mindlessly. We eat for social reasons, emotional reasons and, of course, we eat for the simple pleasure of eating. Eating out is also a form of entertainment. The truth is that there we love our food and while expressing that love we do not necessarily apply the principles of healthy eating or counting calories. Health, nutrition and virtues of food are usually an afterthought. This holds true when we are preoccupied at work. Know your triggers and deal with them, surround yourself with appropriate foods.

Also remember that for mental clarity and focus digestive rest is best. Allow your body to perform at its best by directing your body's energy to your brain rather than your belly. Do not eat oily junk food. Eat small and light comfort foods which are easy to digest. Vegetable juice, salad, fruits, dry fruits, work well, to keep you alert and happy. Following the 5Ps in general will help. This in-fact will help you in stressful situations and even when you are sleep deprived. Avoid overeating and hydrate well. If you have tea coffee ensure you have an additional cup of water for each cup.

HOW TO COPE WITH FOOD COMA

Sitting (Refer to *Read more*, page 307) at the desk at work and struggling to concentrate after about an hour or hour and a half? You are not alone! It happens to the best of us. Welcome to 'food coma'. What causes food coma? Food should not make us feel fatigued, in fact it should be the opposite, that is, we should feel energised. Increased sleepiness is thought to be caused by hormonal and neuro-chemical changes related to both quantity and type of food. The key is obviously in how much we eat and what we eat. Some foods improve energy levels, while others may hinder it. Overeating results in feeling foggy and sluggish. Food coma is often triggered by big meals and high carbohydrate and fat rich meals. The bigger the meal, easier it gets to slip into a food coma. Many scientific studies have also indicated that sleepiness increases after meals and that the extent varies according to the fat and carbohydrate content of the food eaten. High carbohydrate and high glycemic index foods like rice, bread, cakes, cookies, sweets, desserts, fruit juices can cause fluctuations in blood sugar levels. High glycemic foods rapidly break down into glucose, the simplest form of sugar in our body, causing a spike in blood sugar levels. This is followed by a spike in insulin levels (the hormone secreted by the pancreas) to bring down blood sugar levels quickly. The rapid rise in insulin also causes our brain to produce a neurotransmitters serotonin and melatonin (Refer to *Read more,* page 255) that leave us feeling drowsy and sleepy. Wider fluctuations in blood sugar levels increase the fatigue and lethargy. Food coma can also come independent of the composition of the meal, if the meal is large. The response to a larger quantity or volume in the digestive tract triggers – a response to the nervous system to induce sleepiness. Sleepiness due to 'food coma' should not be confused with daytime sleepiness as seen in 'sleep apnoea'.

UNHEALTHY FOOD FOR CONVENIENCE

Sometimes we choose unhealthy junk food simply because it's convenient to eat just like a sandwich or burger like wraps which is easy to pick up, hold and eat as compared to rice, roti, daal and vegetables which are more cumbersome. An easy solution is to have rotis as rolls stuffed with vegetables and meats like wraps or have rice & gravy/ daals & pulse in a bowl. Just like the Chinese and Japanese eat noodles and rice on the go – meals in a bowl.

Some people don't feel very hungry in the morning. So don't force yourself to follow 'eat well since you are breaking the fast'. You could opt for vegetable juice or tea and nuts in the morning and have the main meal when hungry, which could be around 12 pm. Then the next main meal could be around 5–7 pm. One needs to anticipate the flow of the day then plan meals and snacks, accordingly.

Fight the Fog

1. Eat small frequent meals for a steady flow of energy and improving blood sugar metabolism. Practise portion control and avoid eating large meals.

2. Choose the right kind of carbohydrates, protein and good fats in the right proportions. Good fats, protein and fibre are important as they delay the stomach emptying into the intestines, where absorption of nutrients takes place. These will help decrease and slow insulin response and keep you alert and active. Go for whole grains and blended grains and limit intake of sugar, sweets, bakery, biscuits and sweetened beverages.

3. Combine low glycemic index foods with the high glycemic index foods. Example: combine pulses with cereals.

4. Aim to fill most of your half plate with vegetables. Make sure 50% of the vegetables you consume are raw.

5. Take a short walk or stroll after your meal to improve insulin response to the meal.

FOOD SAFETY AT WORK

SAFE COOKWARE AND TIFFIN

As far as possible minimize use of plastic and aluminium. Tiffins ideally should be stainless steel or glass. Utensils used in cooking and heating (Refer to *Read more,* page 292) must not be made of aluminium. (Safe drinking water must be a priority. Wherever possible alkaline water (Refer to *Read more,* page 209) could be introduced.) Minimise use of nonstick pans. The use of microwave ovens, commonly used to reheat food, should be minimised.

Good cooking ware in the kitchen is an integral part of cooking and can have a far reaching impact on health. Cooking ware should be safe, convenient and durable. A variety of materials are used in homes today, some traditional and some modern. The selection is usually dictated by cultures, cuisines and preferences.

IN A NUTSHELL

Generally speaking it's important to plan your diet daily, just the way you plan your dress every morning depending on how your day will be and who all you will be meeting through the day. If there is a client meeting over lunch or dinner, a date, a birthday or a family get together to attend, then it is of utmost importance to plan your meals keeping these in mind to avoid overeating and tipping over your usual day's diet. One must learn to make food swaps to compensate for overeating. Keeping the other meals lighter with vegetables, soups, salads or fruits can definitely help keep your calorie intake in check. At work when we are pre-occupied we may eat much more than we actually should. The important thing to remember is that to lose or, manage weight or belly fat one must watch carbohydrate intake. During travel or when it is difficult to stick to your diet regimen, simply making one meal of fruits or salad is a good idea. Sprouts can also be included in one of the meals and are a good substitute for daals. Try to work with raw vegetables (Refer to *Read more,* page 311), vegetable juices (Refer to *Read more,* page 230), fruits and fluids in the morning.

Add functional foods like aloe juice, amla juice, apple cider vinegar etc. in the morning. A handful of nuts and seeds daily is a good goal (preferably soaked). Another valuable addition to the morning is soaked dry fruits like figs, raisin, sultanas (munakka), prunes, apricots and dry dates. They add valuable fibre and alkalinity to your diet.

PUTTING IT ALL TOGETHER...

Most people at the workplace are struggling to stay in shape. Some are striving to achieve a six pack body while others are looking to get a size zero waist. Here are some tips to achieve your goals in the midst of work pressures, domestic demands and social obligations.

· Try working with no more than two main meals (unless you graze all day).

· These two meals should be according to your peak hunger times and of course fit in with your work, home and social compulsions. Remember not to load up after 7 pm.

· Ensure at least two protein rich meals and pair with vegetables.

Recommended timings

Breakfast	Lunch	Supper/ Dinner
7-10 am	12-3pm	5-7pm/8pm

GET STARTED

· Set goals
· Trim belly fat
· Understand food groups
· Investigate nutritional status and deficiencies
· Listen to your body and look out for food sensitivities
· Maintain a food diary

BE CARB WISE (Cereal)
(Refer to *Read more*, page 310)

· Don't be grain centric : 70% of your diet needs to be plant foods
· Reduce cereals for those trying to lose weight
· Avoid biscuits. Replace with nuts, seeds, dry fruits and makhanas.

· Cutback on added sugars in aerated drinks/ tea/ coffee.

· Lower glycemic index of your diet

· Stop fruit juices. Replace with vegetable juices.

ADD LIVE FOODS

· Dedicate one meal to at least 50% raw vegetables (Refer to *Read more*, page 311), soup, green leafy vegetables daily.

· Include fruits/ sprouts regularly.

· Incorporate lemon or amla daily as they provide (negative calories are enzyme rich)

· Prefer local, seasonal and organic.

ADD HEALTHY FATS

· Use cold pressed oils & cold pressed traditional fats (mustard, sesame, coconut, extra virgin olive (mustard and ghee [clarified butter])

· Say NO to hydrogenated fats.

· Add good fats like omega 3 fats (from flax seeds/ chia seeds/ green leafy vegetables/ fatty fish).

TIME IS KEY

· Avoid cereals after 7 pm.

· Prefer a.m. eating over p.m. eating.

HEALTHY HABITS

· Hydrate well. At-least 2.5-3 litres daily.

· Walk 10000 steps daily.

- Limit salt, caffeine and alcohol (Refer to *Read more*, page 244)
- Oil pulling regularly at least once a week with virgin coconut or mustard oil (improves oral flora and thereby gut flora)
- Ensure intake of special protective foods (aloe, ginger, turmeric, tulsi, probiotics and prebiotics like psylium husk, high fibre foods. 'Remember it is cheaper to eat healthy than fall sick'.
- Go organic – reduce toxins and avoid unwarranted medication
- Chew well
- Ensure good sleep
- Follow an active lifestyle, practice yoga and meditation
- Keep a positive outlook. Don't take failure to your heart & success to your head.

"Healthy eating is the best investment for a productive life."

SUGGESTED DIET PLAN

Protective Foods		
Super foods	Aloevera, Amla, Apple cider vinegar, Lemon, Ginger	Pick as many
Leaves	Tulsi, Mint , Wheat grass	Pick as many
Spices	Cumin, Coriander, Aniseed, Carom seeds, Cloves, Black pepper, Organic Turmeric, Cinnamon	Pick as many
Nuts and seeds	Almond, Walnut, Cashew, Pistachio, Chiraita, Flax seeds, Chia seeds, Sunflowers, Pumpkin, Melons	Pick as many
Dry fruits	Raisins, Figs, Dates, Prunes	

3 times grain meal, 2 times protein, 1 meal dedicated to protective foods

Breakfast

Stuffed daal parantha/ Daal poha with vegetables/ Upma with vegetables/ Sundal/ Idli/ Dosa/ Uttapam/ Chilla/ Moong idli/ Sprouts/ Egg + Toast + Vegetables juice + 1 Fruit

Mid-morning

Fruit / Coconut water

Lunch

Salad, Vegetables, Daal / Fish / Chicken, Roti (1-2) / Rice (½ -1 cup)

Evening

Tea / Coffee / Green tea, Roasted namkeen / Chana / Makhana/ Peanuts

Dinner (7:30pm)

Salad /Soup, Vegetables, Roti (1) / Rice (½ cup) / Toast (1)

2 times grain meal, 2 times protein, 1 meal dedicated to protective foods

Breakfast

Fruits

Chilla/ Moong Idlis/ Sprouts (1cup) / Chana-chaat/ Chana-tikki/ Dhokla/ Khandvi/ Egg + Vegetable Juice

Mid-morning

Coconut water/ Green tea

Lunch

Salad, Vegetables, Sprouts

Evening

Tea / Coffee / Green Tea, Roasted Namkeen / Chana / Makhana/ Peanuts

Dinner (7:30pm)

Salad, Vegetables, Daal/ Pulse/ Fish/ Chicken, Roti (1-2) / Rice (½ -1 cup)

1 grain meal, 2 times protein, one meal dedicated to protective foods

---

Breakfast

Fruits

Chilla / Moong idli/ Sprouts (1cup) / Chana chaat / Chana tikki / Dhokla / Khandvi / Egg, Toast / Egg, Roti (1)

Mid-morning

Fruit / Coconut water

Lunch

Salad, Vegetables, Sprouts

Evening

Tea / Coffee / Green tea, Roasted namkeen /Chana /Makhana/ Peanuts

Dinner (7:30pm)

Salad, Vegetables, Soup, Daal / Pulse / Paneer / Chicken / Fish

---

1 grain meal (at devil's hour), 2 times protein, dedicated one meal to protective foods

---

Breakfast

Fruit (1), Vegetables Juice

Mid-morning
Lemon Water / Butter milk / Green Tea

Lunch
Salad, Vegetables, Daal/ Pulse/ Fish/ Chicken

Evening
Tea/ Coffee/ Green Tea, Roasted Namkeen/ Chana/ Makhana/ Peanuts

5:00-7:00pm
Tea/ Coffee/ Green Tea
Roti Roll/ Wraps/ Sandwich/ Chilla/ Poha with Vegetables/ Pasta/ Burger/ Dosa/ Idli

Dinner (7:30pm)
Green tea
Salad/ Vegetables/ Fruits/ Nuts

---

0 grain diet, 2 times protien, 1 meal dedicated to protective foods

---

Breakfast
Chilla/ Moong Idlis/ Sprouts (1cup)/ Chana-chaat/ Chana-tikki/ Dhokla/ Khandvi

Mid-morning
Fruit / Coconut Water

Lunch
Salad, Vegetables, Soup

Evening
Tea/ Coffee/ Green Tea, Roasted Namkeen/ Chana/ Makhana/ Peanuts

Dinner (7:30pm)
Salad, Vegetables, Soup, Daal / Pulse / Paneer / Chicken / Fish

Detox diet: (Great for balancing excesses and late night eating)

Breakfast

Fruits

Mid-morning

Vegetable Juice / Lemon Water

Lunch

Salad, Sprouts

Evening

Tea/ Coffee/ Green Tea, Roasted Namkeen/ Chana/ Makhana/ Peanuts

Dinner (7:30pm)

Soup, Steamed or Grilled or Stir-fried vegetables / Vegetable Tikki

---

TRICKS OF EACH TRADE

TRIMMING THE OCCUPATIONAL HAZARDS

Every occupation has a unique environment where generalisation does not work. There are granular solutions for different work environments. However, there is a common thread across all professions and trades – it is stress and it has a negative relationship with healthy eating. In this chapter, we have listed out tricks for people, to eat well, irrespective of their professions.

Though the principles of a good, wholesome diet remain consistently general, they need to be tweaked and tempered according to professions, situations and environments. Following a few tips and some smart moves can ensure that no damage is done.

BAKERS/ CHEFS/ TASTERS/ CATERERS/ RESTAURANT AND SWEET SHOP OWNERS

As their profession demands working with food, they have to manage their eating habits more carefully. For those with a positive family history of diabetes, controlling sugar and grains/ cereals is critical.

Some tips to be followed include:

· Learn and practice portion control.

· Maintain a food diary and track your caloric intake.

· Account for every bite that you taste as approx. 25 Kcals.

· Keep to one main meal with grain a day, preferably before 8:00 pm.

· Engage in regular physical activity.

· Minimize alcohol intake.

· Address your food allergies / sensitivities. If you are sensitive to some foods like nuts, gluten (Refer to *Read more*, page 260) or dairy, strictly avoid them. Have colleagues do the tasting.

· Check out nutritional deficiencies and get routine medical checkups.

EX-SPORTSMEN/ EX-DANCERS / EX-SERVICEMEN

People who have led active lifestyles are at high risk of gaining weight after they reduce or stop the physical activity. Mostly, eating habits remain the same leading to a gradual piling-up of pounds. High intensity exercise also creates a leaky gut and chances of food sensitivities.

· Those with a family history of diabetes are more at risk and should watch their weight and waist.
· Cut down portions to adjust to lower physical activity.
· Check for food sensitivities through blood tests if you suffer from a chronic disorder.
· Engage in some form of physical activity like yoga and walking
· Minimize alcohol intake.
· Check for nutritional deficiencies.

CORPORATE EXECUTIVES AND BUREAUCRATS

This group is prone to prolonged sitting, stress, along with consumption of sweets and snacks the effects of which are worsened with smoking.
· Plan your meals.
· Try to eat regular meals. In other words, do not skip meals and avoid long gaps between two meals. For executives, small meals with light snacks work better. Else practice intermittent fasting (Refer to *Read more,* page 273).
· Do not skip breakfast. (Unless you are not hungry)

· As far as possible eat a light lunch. Try a salad, soup, sprouts, beans, lean meats, nuts, yogurt and fruit lunch. It will prevent food coma – keep you more energized and see you through longer.

· Prefer homemade food on a day-to-day basis over cafeteria food.

· Snack smart and say no to trans-fat laden deep fried fatty snacks such as samosas, patties, bread pakoras, fried namkeens, biscuits in meetings.

· Say yes to fresh fruits, nuts, seeds, dry fruits like raisins, prunes, roasted whole grains, puffed rice (murmura), roasted chana and makhanas (lotus seeds).

· Limit or avoid sugar-laden beverages – nimbu pani, aam panna, iced teas, fruit-based beverages. Infused herbal preparations are healthier. If you are dairy intolerant, ensure almond or coconut milk are available else you can have black tea, black coffee, cold brewed coffee.

· If you are obliged to share tea, coffee frequently over meetings, go for green, white or matcha tea (Refer to *Read more,* page 223), herbal spice teas, camomile, jasmine etc., preferably without sugar. Limit portions of tea, coffee to half cup and watch the sugar.

· Limit alcohol to no more than 2 small drinks on any particular day.

· Make time for exercise. Find an opportunity to take short brisk walks within your office complex intermittently during the day. This will increase efficiency and work output.

· Aim to exercise regularly for 60 minutes on most days of the week. Brisk walking, swimming, jogging, dancing, cycling, are some examples of good exercise.

· Meditation and yoga can help you stay relaxed, sharp and focussed.

· Undergo routine medical checkups.

NIGHT SHIFTS/ERRATIC WORKING HOURS/ DELAYED WORKING HOURS/ GRAVE YARD SHIFT

(Refer to *Read more,* page 255)

(Any working hours outside of the typical 9 a.m. – 5 p.m. is considered shift work)

Eating late into the night can disturb hormonal balance and predispose one to developing obesity, high blood pressure, diabetes and other chronic diseases. Night shift workers have a 10% higher risk of developing diabetes.

· Eat small frequent meals and eat your better meal during the day or before 8 pm. Alternatively intermittent fasting (Refer to *Read more,* page 273) is a good option.

· Snack healthy. Avoid having high carbohydrate snacks later in the day or at night.

· Avoid unhealthy food at workplace, especially at night.

· Watch alcohol intake.

· Engage in regular physical activity and yoga.

· Undergo routine medical checkups.

THE FOODIE

The person who loves food can develop an unhealthy relationship with it. While most of us eat for pleasure and hunger, living to eat can become a problem.

· Choose one meal in a day where you eat what you wish to within your grains/cereal allowance.
· Write a food diary to track your portions.
· Engage in regular physical exercise.
· Limit alcohol intake.
· If need be, seek professional assistance to address compulsive eating patterns or emotional eating.
· Look out for food sensitivities or get yourself evaluated for nutritional deficiencies, if you are perpetually hungry.

HOMEMAKERS

Women who stay at home are so busy making life comfortable for the rest of the family that they have no time for themselves within the confines of the house. Moreover, they have easy access to food leading to unwarranted snacking. The usual outings or me-time activities are also usually coffee mornings, lunches, movies or shopping. Most of these activities are food-centric too.

Keep the following checks and balances in mind when eating out:
· Plan your day around the coffee mornings or lunches and

keep other meals light and do not go overboard.

· If you over-indulge, balance out the excesses in the following meal or on the following day by exercising a little extra or walking that extra mile or by having lighter meals centred around fruits and vegetables.

· Try to eat your dinner early, by about 7:00-7:30 pm on most days. Even if you are alone, soon the family will follow.

DOCTORS AND HEALTHCARE PROFESSIONALS

One would imagine them to be most clued in as far as their diets are concerned. However, the reality is that barring some, most are far away from healthy eating. This may be due to paucity of time or a lack of focus on food due to preoccupation with patient care. In either case, they are mouthpieces for healthy diet advice and therefore must walk the talk.

A doctor or healthcare professional must look healthy and fit to inspire patients. It is important to plan the day:

· The morning regime should be dedicated to live foods – sprouts, special protective foods like aloevera, honey, lemon, vegetable juices, smoothies, soaked nuts, seeds, spiced water and herbs etc.

· Add proteins such as lentils (dal or besan chillas, stir-fried chick peas, moong dal idlis, dal dosas, dhoklas), eggs, pulses (lentil snacks).

· Grains / cereals in the form of muesli, toast, quinoa, rice flakes, idli, dosas, can be included according to individual needs.

· Given the paucity of time and the endless stream of

patients and visitors, ideally take a five minute break to have your snack or meal.

· Lunch whether on the go or sit down must include vegetables and protiens. If there is no time, keep roasted channas, nuts or daals, puffed rice, soups, vegetable juices, coconut water, lemon water, tea or coffee handy.

· OPDs and evening clinics get in the way of evening tea. However, as hunger strikes, almost universally with maximum impact at this time, it is imperative to eat sensibly between 5-7 pm. It is a good idea to carry two tiffins. Have a grain / cereal in the form of a roti roll, idli or sandwich or meal in a bowl to refuel yourself. Remember cereals after 7 pm are discouraged, from health, weight and longevity (Refer to *Read more*, page 277) perspectives.

· Check for nutritional deficiencies.

PILOTS AND CABIN CREW

Pilots and cabin crew are exposed to radiations in the form of solar flares. According to research, a single trans Atlantic flight from east to west can expose them to radiations equivalent to several X-rays.

Recent reports highlight an increase in the incidence of certain kinds of cancer among airline pilots and cabin crew. Renewed concerns about possible exposure to harmful levels of cosmic radiation at high altitudes have been raised. Till more conclusive evidence is established precaution is prudent.

· To reduce oxidative stress strictly avoid smoking and limit alcohol intake.

· Take special anti-inflammatory foods – functional foods and omega-3 rich foods.

· Increase enzyme rich foods – sprouts, smoothies, green leafy vegetables.

· Limit intake of sugar and processed foods.

· Address nutritional deficiencies, if any.

· Stay well hydrated.

· Avoid excess tea and coffee.

· Intermittent fasting and detox diets are certainly a good way to get rid of excessive free radicals and associated damage.

· Address nutritional deficiencies including Vitamin D.

(To know more about Jet-lag refer to *Read more,* page 300)

ACTORS, ARTISTS, CELEBRITIES, PUBLIC AND POLITICAL FIGURES

· Depending on the location and schedules carry the essential part of the diet like live and cleansing foods – sprouts, vegetable juices, special protective foods like aloevera, honey, lemon, soaked nuts and seeds etc – with you. You may have some of these in the morning or before the shoot or performance.

· Those having special dietary requirements should carry packed food. Inform organisers about these.

· Have plenty of fluids like coconut water for hydration. Keep your special teas or infusion bags, if you can.

· Make sure your supplements accompany you as travel is an integral part of life.

JOURNALISTS AND LAWYERS

These people have long hours of work and demanding schedules where no amount of planning can be enough.

• Breakfast or first meal should include fresh vegetable juices, fruits; protein in the form of eggs, sprouts, chillas. A healthy grain/ cereal if needed can be added.

• Smart snacks like nuts, channa, sprouts, fruits can be packed for travel or office.

• At meal times, most people manage lentils, dals, vegetables and grains/ cereals. It is the evening or snacking where things go horribly off! Snack smart in the evenings (devil's hour).

• Plan to eat most of your grain/ cereal or your main meal between 5-7 pm.

• Practice weekly fasting or detox diets.

• Undergo routine medical check-ups.

LECTURERS AND TEACHERS

They are on their feet mostly and need to fill up, especially at mid-day / lunch time:

• Breakfast can be variable as per need but a post school / college meal after a full day is a must. The satisfaction of the meal has to be high as it meets requirements for hunger and comfort.

• Dinner can be light with or without a grain/cereal for weight watchers. Evening snack before 7 pm may can include grain/cereal.

· Extra eating or late night eating through celebrations, meetings, which are almost a regular feature, must be accounted for.

· Address nutritional deficiencies

SMART EATING TIPS FOR WOMEN IN THE WORK FORCE

Women face more trauma through the reproductive ages and hormonal changes during their life cycle compared to men. These changes coupled with work and domestic demands take a toll on their health and make them more vulnerable to developing nutritional deficiencies, and health problems.

YOUNG MOTHERS

Always short on time and on-the-go, young mothers never have the time to think about their meals or activities. Make it a point to make time for yourself.

· Do not be the scavenger – resist the temptation to eat your child's leftovers. That waste will soon be on your waist.

· Keep a food dairy (Refer to *Read more,* page 289).

· Make time for exercise even if for short spells – socialize with health conscious friends.

· Meet over coffee / tea rather than meals.

· Develop and share healthy recipes.

· Address nutritional deficiencies

PREGNANT WOMEN

Most pregnant women are told to eat well as they are eating for two. This is not necessary. Eat well and eat healthy to gain the right amount of weight during pregnancy (8-12 kgs).

· Calorie needs during the first three months are similar to that of a non-pregnant woman. During the second and third trimesters, energy needs are increased by 15% only. Add good quality proteins and carbohydrates to your diet. Include omega 3 fats – walnuts, fish, seafood, flax-seeds, mustard seeds, sesame seeds and dark green leafy vegetables prior to conception and throughout pregnancy.

· Include iron rich foods – especially lean meats, poultry eggs and fish, black gram (kala chana), green leafy vegetables, water melon and dry fruits like sultanas, dates, raisins, prunes, figs, apricots.

· Vitamin C also helps in iron absorption. Include citrus fruits like oranges, lemon, guava, amla and tomatoes. Cook in iron vessels.

· Increased need for some vitamins and minerals is important – calcium, magnesium, folic acid, zinc and some B-vitamins. Include these under professional guidance.

Peri & Post Menopause

Women in pre-menopausal and post menopausal phase often complain of increasing girth and sugar cravings. Many complain of hot flushes, night sweats, mood swings, depression, anxiety, sleep issues and dryness in their bodies. Certain lifestyle changes can help:

· Choose low glycemic index foods, reduce sugar intake, and avoid eating late.

· Beneficial at this stage are foods rich in antioxidants, vitamins, minerals and fatty acids. It is common to develop nutritional deficiencies, which must be corrected

· Useful additions to the diet are also green tea, wheat grass, aloevera, basil, turmeric, cinnamon and black cohosh.

· This is the time when the gut undergoes changes which sets the stage for losing intolerance to foods like gluten and dairy.

· Undergo routine medical check-ups.

MANAGE STRESS

Stress and emotions can make you eat mindlessly. The key is to learn the difference between physiological and psychological hunger. Some stress is needed to perform but chronic stress can take a toll on health. Focusing on your attitude, social network, community, spiritual beliefs, and sense of purpose can have an impact on your stress levels and managing these aspects of your life has actually been associated with dramatic reductions in disease and increased longevity. (Dr. Mark Hymne)

Some practical tips to manage stress include:

· Avoid over eating when fatigued or too stressed. Try drinking water instead.

• Be optimistic and keep a positive attitude.

• 5–10 minutes (any time of the day) of regular meditation can help you gain control and clarity of thoughts.

• Deep breathing exercises anywhere, even on your office seat or while you are in the car, can help you relax and calm your nerves.

• 10–15 minutes of yoga including 'asanas' and 'pranayam' (breathing) can help attain control of mind and body.

• Prayer, bio-feedback, neuro-feedback, hypnotherapy and pursuit of your hobbies are useful techniques.

• Practice time management.

• Avoid excessive caffeine, alcohol and tobacco. Stay well hydrated. Dehydration can trigger anxiety and confusion.

• Try and get 6-8 hours of sleep daily.

• Spend at least 1 hour/day with family.

• Take regular breaks/weekends. Try to holiday every 3 months with family.

• Massage can have a rejuvenating effect.

• Listening to relaxing music is therapeutic and calming.

• Consider having a pet. Stroking an animal has been found to help relax.

• Learn to recognize your own threshold for stress and do not push yourself past it.

• Look out for food sensitivity. Pay attention to gut

health and correct nutritional deficiencies. Adding probiotics, magnesium, and B vitamins along with good fats (omega-3 and coconut) is useful.

TIFFIN OR PACKED LUNCH

The age old tiffin or home packed tiffin box/ tiffin carrier (dabba) has been replaced by cafeteria and office kitchen food. Number of eateries outside the office space has grown considerably. The dabbawalas in many cities in India have also become an integral force in feeding urban office goers. Mostly these are full meals like lentil / pulses, vegetables and grains/ cereals. In case you are trying to reserve the grains/cereals for the peak hunger time (5-7 pm), in which case you can have lentils and vegetables at lunch time. Ensure you include some raw vegetables including carrots, cucumber, nuts and fruits in your tiffin/ packed lunch.

HOW TO SUSTAIN WHAT
HAS BEEN STARTED

Once you have mastered the 'planning' of the ultimate diet plan, with the 5Ps, understood what to eat, when to eat and how to eat, it is imperative to keep doing it in ad infinitum. That might be a scary thought at first, but very doable and well worth it. It might be a good idea to pin up a checklist in your cubicle or work area.

When it becomes overwhelming or challenging to keep to the checklist or be mindful all the time, don't panic and don't give up. Balance out the excesses by eating fruits, vegetables, sprouts etc. Going back to what we said initially – it is about mindful eating.

MINDFUL EATING

(Refer to *Read more*, page 297)

THINGS TO DO

- Maintain a food diary.

· Increase awareness.

· Learn the difference between physiological and psychological hunger.

· Pay attention to what you choose. You may still be overloading on calories even if you have left out most of that buffet!

· Ensure intake of special foods for well-being such as aloevera, ginger, turmeric, tulsi, probiotics, prebiotics.

· Focus on your food. Don't eat while making a presentation or a sales pitch. Carve out at least 15-20 minutes to savour what you have on your plate. It will keep you feeling satiated for a longer time. Chew well.

· When entertaining a client, at a conference or on a retreat, pre-plate your food. Put all that you want to eat at one go. Most people tend to eat less if they put everything on their plate like in a 'Traditional Thali' or the Japanese 'Bento Box' and are able to see how much they are going to eat (eating with eyes). The brain takes about 20 minutes to signal fullness. However, those individuals who like to be busy with food for longer, should go in for smaller portions and if need be go for second and third servings. According to same studies, people eat about 14% less when they take smaller amounts and go back for seconds and thirds.

• Portion control: We psychologically use counting as a yardstick to judge how much we have eaten.

• Use smaller plates and bowls.

• Make smaller sized idlis, cutlets, tikkis, rotis etc.

• Have an appropriate option for that time when your colleague orders a pizza and the whole office smells like a pizzeria.

• Do not compare yourself with others. Remember you are unique.

• Pay attention to how you are feeling. Your moods can affect your food intake. People often eat when they are tired, angry, upset, lonely, or bored. Find the proper activity to deal with the specific feeling – eating is not it!

If you are tired, take a catnap or go for a walk; if you are angry talk with a friend, write in your journal, or do something you love to do. When you are bored, make a phone call to someone you have not spoken with for a long time, or make a list of all the things you have put off doing. Learn to cope with emotional eating and boredom. Drinking water and staying hydrated helps.

• Avoid grains/cereals in the beginning of the meal, chances are you will end up eating too much of it. Start with soup, salad and vegetables, and delay the grains/cereals to the end of the meal. It will help you limit intake of grains/cereals and be well within your grains/ cereal allowance.

· Keep your home stocked with fruits and vegetables.

· Don't drink water during a meal, at best take small sips. Ideally drink an hour before or after meals. Take adequate fluids during the day.

· Eat frequently. Divide your food intake into three main meals and two snacks. Though not etched in stone, it is desirable. Avoid large meals particularly at night as they promote weight gain and digestive disturbances.

· 'Don't waste' is a noble dictum. But excess food goes either to waste or to the waist – certainly not to the needy!

· Don't use food as reward or punishment.

· Do not keep food too accessible if you are a compulsive eater. Seek professional help, if needed.

· Identify your cravings or discuss with your nutritionist. You may have food sensitivities or nutritional deficiencies.

· You must look forward to your meals. Make your meals enjoyable. Try out different cuisines.

· Eat something that you like once a day, ideally at the peak hunger time.

· Choose healthy sweets. If possible, replace sweets with a fruit.

· Choose low calorie healthy beverages. Make interesting vegetable juices, smoothies, and soups.

· Late night fixes can be dark chocolate, hot chocolate,

To reiterate it's all about planning.

A) Plan your meals and snacks in advance. Snack smart.

B) Most social activities are around food, so plan your day accordingly.

C) Start your day with breakfast and choose a low glycemic index breakfast.

D) Eat your favourite food once a week.

E) Keep indulgence to no more than one meal a week and do not go overboard. Watch your weekend indulgence. Often, people who do very well throughout the week let go on the weekend, often leading to weight gain on Monday mornings. Detox or practice fasting.

F) Make diet changes that can be maintained for life.

G) Quick fixes are counter-productive for healthy weight management.

H) Travel smart

I) Follow the principles of your diet during your holidays too (Refer to *Read more,* page 304) bhuna channa, seeds, nuts and some fruits.

· Maintain a healthy kitchen: Use pressure cookers, slow cookers, steamers and juicers, air fryers, grills, healthy cookware.

· Watch out for temptation — Eating with your eyes. (Refer to *Read more,* page 297)

SHOP AND STOCK SMART

· Plan your shopping in advance. Be a smart shopper and read food labels to help you make the right choices.

· Buy and stock appropriate snacks like nuts, seeds, fresh fruits, vegetables and roasted snacks.

· Avoid storing unhealthy foods on a regular basis.

· Learn to read labels. Do not simply buy on the basis of claims like 'fat-free', 'sugar-free' or 'cholesterol-free'. Reading nutrition labels helps you to get a sense of whether a particular food is healthy. Avoid labels which have ingredients in codes. You do not understand as these are surely not natural. Also avoid labels which have too many ingredients. Chances are they are loaded with too many chemicals. Watch out for hidden sugars on food labels.

· Choose organic wherever possible: Use organic/locally grown foods. Organic is no longer a fashion statement or a fad. Indiscriminate use of fertilisers and pesticides has resulted in a number of health hazards. Consumed on a regular basis, these chemicals form deposits in our tissues and vital organs, particularly liver, kidney, and brain. As the years progress, they lead to life threatening diseases and even cancer – reason why they are "cumulative poisons". Organic food is grown without pesticides and chemical inputs. Consuming locally and regionally grown foods too is a more sensible approach as it ensures that food is fresh, more nutritious, has fewer "travel miles" and less handling or processing. Growing your own produce in your own pots, gardens or farms is the best way to ensure that the fruits and vegetables you eat are pesticide free.

EXERCISE AND SLEEP

A good diet along with meditation and physical activity ensures complete wellness.

Engage in regular physical activity in some form for at least 45 minutes on most days of the week. It can be yoga, breathing exercises, brisk walk or a sport that you enjoy and does not have to be an ultra-endurance event or competitive sports.

· Sitting (Refer to *Read more,* page 307) is the new tobacco. De-addict by moving around your office, go up and down the stairs or ask for a standing desk.

· Pre- and post-gym exercise, hydrate yourself well, drink enough fluids – salted lemon water, coconut water or have a fruit.

· If you are doing light weights, ensure you have a combination of protein and carbohydrate snacks like milk shakes, smoothies, egg and milk or a cheese / chicken / egg sandwich as soon as you finish.

· Get adequate good quality sleep, atleast 6–8 hours.

MANAGE STRESS

Dietary changes can help manage stress. Some foods such as chocolate, seeds and nuts, bananas, dates and mangoes have a calming effect. Eliminating inflammatory foods like wheat, barley, oats, rye, soy and corn in people with food sensitivities can help improve moods.

REGULAR HEALTH-CHECKS AND FOLLOW-UPS

Go for annual health check-ups. These should include a thorough physical examination, blood pressure measurement, blood glucose level, fasting lipid profile, body composition, along with a thorough assessment of nutritional deficiencies, dietary and exercise habits, and assessment of stress levels.

If you have chronic health complaints, mood disorders, are unable to get rid of excess weight, look out for food intolerances and seek professional help. Remember, most diseases begin in the gut.

If all is well such check-ups should be done at least once in 2 years. If any abnormality is found, frequent follow ups are desirable.

IDENTIFY PROBLEM AREAS

Keep a tab on your diet, exercise, thoughts and habits like addiction, cravings, alcohol, eating disorders, moods and relationships, which conflict with your health goals. Work on these to apply corrections and seek professional help, if necessary.

SEEKING SUPPORT

· Good eating habits are infectious. You should take the lead and be an example for your family and friends.

· Involve your family and seek their support when possible.

· Do not succumb to social pressures. Learn the art of saying 'NO'. Ask for desirable alternatives.

· Make technology your friend. Use the various apps available today such as theweightmonitor.com to track your food intake and manage your weight and health. After all, what we can measure we can manage!

WHAT WORKPLACES CAN DO

While most organizations and even governments agree that employee nutrition is very important, workplace nutrition is not a top concern for them. Many take nutrition for granted and have more pressing issues to deal with, according to the

International Labour Organization (ILO).

Most large companies have meal programmes or a canteen but the attitude is that if workers don't like the food served, they are free to bring a packed lunch or buy it elsewhere. Very little thought or investment is given to the subject.

At a workplace don't worry about the work done, focus on nourishing the worker, and the work will automatically happen, says Sadhguru JaggiVasudev.

Echoing the thought, ILO says that good nutrition is the foundation of workplace productivity, safety, job security and it is shared by governments, employers, trade unions and workers. For example, iron deficiency, affects up-to half of the world's population, predominantly in the developing world. Low iron levels are associated with weakness, sluggishness and lack of coordination. Ensuring that workers have enough iron (or calories, in general) will lead to greater productivity and reduce accidents. This in turn leads to higher profits for the company, leading to higher wages and better job security.

It also says that in industrialized countries, one of the highest business costs is health care. Sick days, long-term absences and the general drain on productivity are due to chronic diseases or obesity, to name a few.

Employers must understand that proper nutrition leads to higher productivity, so nutrition is a wise investment. Merely providing a meal programme or access to food can be counterproductive if that food is not nutritious. Good nutrition makes a stronger, better-equipped workforce that, in the long run, will make their company and country more competitive and more attractive to investors. Workplaces should have registered nutritionist on board to help guide and monitor employee's health and food services.

Without a foundation of good workplace nutrition, many other hard-fought benefits become meaningless. A good medical plan will be pushed to the limit if workers are sick from poor nutrition. Retirement benefits are not useful if the worker dies of a stroke or heart attack by the retirement age. Job security is impossible to guarantee when sick workers and malnourished children crush national productivity and investment. Governments, employers, workers and their organizations together must capitalize on the opportunity to use the workplace as a platform to promote nutrition in order to reap the rewards that this so clearly yields: health, safety, productivity, economic growth and a civil society.

Employee Wellness Programmes have become a staple in many corporations as a way to attract top talent, keep them happy and productive and decrease employee turnover. The key to having a successful Corporate Wellness programme is by encouraging overall well-being while still keeping it fun. Education and awareness followed with alternatives is key to change.

SOUND INVESTMENTS TO A HEALTHY BALANCE SHEET

• Provide your employees with healthy office snacks and a healthy pantry. Healthy snacks aid in weight control, improve the mood and boost energy.

• Office meetings must avoid biscuits, samosas, sandwiches or other unhealthy carbohydrate or sugar laden foods. Replace these with roasted, plain, salted nuts, channa, fresh fruits or vegetables sticks. Tea and coffee (Refer to *Read more,* page 220) can be replaced with infused water or green tea.

• Create a healthy office cookbook. Ask employees to share their favourite healthy recipes – compile the best ones into a collection and share with colleagues and families.

• Bring in an expert or a chef to demonstrate easy, healthy cooking and share recipes.

• Vegetables and fruit smoothies and salad competitions should be conducted in office as an activity to promote health and wellness.

• Address special needs of vegan, gluten and dairy etc. for those who are intolerant to them. If possible provide alkaline water. (Refer to *Read more,* page 209)

• Put up a wellness wall. Share the health success stories.

• Publish a workplace wellness newsletter.

• Hold a health fair.

• Discourage smoking.

• Create standing desks wherever possible.

• Introduce yoga and gyms if possible.

• Promote laughter by having laughter clubs or comedy shows or simply providing them tickets for comedy shows.

• Sponsor a company retreat or off-site around sports.

• Incentivize through executive health check-ups, weight loss goals, gym memberships and wellness gadgets.

QUICK AND EASY
RECIPES FOR
LIFELONG HEALTH

CONTENTS

Smoothies and Beverages (protective foods)

32. Green Lemonade
33. Citrus Margarita Cooler
34. Chocolate Peanut Butter Smoothie
35. Fruit smoothie
36. Vegetables juice
37. Coconut milk curd

Salad Dressings

38. Basic Dressing for Greens
39. Healthy Mayo
40. Lemon Dressing
41. Simple Vinaigrette
42. Balsamic Almond Dressing

Salads

43. Broccoli 'n' Sesame salad (protective foods)
44. Papaya and Beetroot Salad (protective foods)
45. Fruit 'n' Nut Coleslaw Salad (protective foods)
46. Indian Chickpea Salad (protien)
47. Burrito Bowl with Cauliflower Rice (protective foods)
48. Roasted Sweet Potato (cereal/grain)
49. Farro Salad (cereal/grain)

Soups

50. Chicken soup (protien)
51. Mushroom soup (protective foods)
52. Tomato Basil soup (protective foods)
53. Spinach soup (protective foods)

Vegetarian Mains

54. Lemon rice (cereal/grain)
55. Fried Rice (cereal/grain)
56. Buddha Bowl (cereal/grain)

Non-vegetarian Mains

57. Chicken with peanut butter (protien)

Wraps

58. Asian Chicken Lettuce Wraps (protien paired with vegetables)
59. Collard Wrap Bento Boxes

Desserts

60. Flour-less Griddle Cake
61. Chia Seeds Pudding
62. Best Chocolate Cake

BREAKFAST AND SNACKS

FRESH FRUIT NUT OATMEAL

SERVES: 2

INGREDIENTS

1 ½ cups water

¼ tsp cinnamon

⅓ cup old fashioned or steel cut oats

2 tbsp raisins or currants

1 cup fresh or frozen berries such as blueberries

1 banana, sliced

1 apple, peeled, cored, and chopped or grated

2 tbsp chopped walnuts

If you use steel cut oats, increase cooking time to 20 minutes or until oats are tender.

METHOD

1. In a medium saucepan, combine the water, cinnamon, oats, and currants. Simmer until the oatmeal is creamy.

2. Add the berries and sliced banana.

3. Cook for 5 minutes, or until hot, stirring constantly. Mix in the apple and nuts.

CINNAMON-SPICED BAKED OATMEAL

SERVES: 3

INGREDIENTS

1 cup old fashioned oats

⅓ cup raisins or chopped, unsulfured dried apricots

2 dates chopped

2 tbsp ground flax-seeds

1 cup unsweetened soy, hemp or almond milk

⅔ cup water

1 tsp vanilla extract

1 tsp cinnamon or pumpkin pie spice

½ cup fresh or thawed frozen blueberries or any other sweet seasonal fruit

METHOD

1. Place all the Ingredients in a large bowl and stir to combine. Grease a 7 x10 pan. Pour the oatmeal mixture into the pan and cover with lid or foil.

2. Place in the refrigerator overnight.

3. In the morning uncover the pan and place in a cold oven.

4. Bake at 350 degree Fahrenheit for 18-20 minutes.

Properly stored, cooked oatmeal will last for 4-6 days in the refrigerator.

BUCKWHEAT CREAMY PORRIDGE

SERVES: 2-4

INGREDIENTS

½ cup buckwheat groats (100 grams)

2 cup unsweetened plant milk of your choice or oat milk.

2 bananas

Toppings: cacao nibs, maple syrup, sliced almonds or almond butter.

METHOD

1. Soak buckwheat groats for at least 4 hours. This makes buckwheat groats easier to digest and cooks them faster.

2. Drain the groats and add them to a food processor or a blender with the milk. Blend until smooth.

3. Add the mixture to a saucepan, bring to a boil and cook for 5 minutes over medium-high heat. Stirring occasionally.

4. Keep leftovers in a sealed container in the fridge for up-to 4 days.

QUINOA POWER BREAKFAST BOWL

SERVES: 2

INGREDIENTS

½ cup quinoa uncooked

1 and a quarter cup of almond milk (unsweetened)

1 tsp ground cinnamon

1 tbsp maple syrup or honey

1 tbsp almond butter

FOR TOPPINGS

1 banana (sliced)

¼ cup sliced almonds

¼ cup coconut flakes (fresh, unsweetened)

METHOD

1. Add quinoa and almond milk into a small saucepan. Bring the mixture to a boil, then reduce to simmer and cook for 15 minutes, stirring occasionally until it's creamy and the quinoa is cooked. Stir in almond butter and maple syrup.

2. Transfer to two bowls and top with sliced banana, sliced almond and coconut flakes.

3. Store in the refrigerator for up-to 2 days.

BERRY "YOGURT"

SERVES: 4

INGREDIENTS

250 grams frozen mixed berries or fresh berries such as blueberries, strawberry, gooseberry and blackberries.

250 grams 0 percent - fat Greek yogurt

1 tbsp honey or agave syrup

METHOD

1. Blend yogurt, berries and honey or agave syrup in a food processor for 20 seconds, until it comes together as a smooth ice-cream texture.

2. Scoop into a bowl and chill. Can be stored up-to 1 month.

FRUITY CHICKPEA CEREAL

SERVES: 2

INGREDIENTS

1 cup boiled and steamed chickpea

2 bananas sliced

1 bowl of mixed fruits (kiwi, dragon-fruit, apple, berries, pear, watermelon etc)

1 cup almond milk

2 tsp honey

METHOD

1. Divide the chickpeas in two cereal bowls. Place bananas on top of the beans. Refrigerate for 10 minutes to chill.

2. Add berries or any other fruits. Add the almond milk and honey when serving. Otherwise store for up-to 2 days.

CREAMY BREAKFAST BROCCOLI

SERVES: 4

INGREDIENTS

½ cup raw bacon (about 4-6 slices) chopped into small pieces (optional)

1 tbsp butter

4-5 cloves garlic minced or crushed

3 cups broccoli florets

½ teaspoon garlic powder

½ teaspoon crushed red pepper optional

Salt and pepper to taste

1 cup heavy cream or light cream or half and half

½ cup shredded mozzarella or cheddar, or your favorite melting cheese

¼ cup Parmesan cheese (optional)

METHOD

1. Pre-heat oven to 400F. In a large pan over medium-high heat, cook chopped bacon for 2-3 minutes or until almost crispy.

2. Remove bacon from pan and to the same pan, add the butter, garlic, broccoli, garlic powder, crushed red pepper and a dash of salt and pepper.

3. Sautee for 2-3 minutes or until the garlic is fragrant. Add the heavy cream, cheese, and cooked bacon.

4. Transfer to preheated oven and cook for 12-15 minutes or until the cheese is bubbly and the broccoli is cooked to desired doneness. Eat as a main meal or as a side.

TOFU SCRAMBLE WITH TOMATOES AND BELL PEPPERS

SERVES: 2

INGREDIENTS

1 tbsp olive oil

200 grams block firm tofu

½ small red onion, chopped

1 tsp turmeric

¼ cup water

1 tbsp soy cuisine (optional), you can also use almond butter instead or just leave it out

1 tsp soy sauce

1 pinch kala namak (Himalayan salt)

Black pepper, to taste

1 large tomato

METHOD

1. Use a fork or hands to crumble the tofu into small pieces. In a medium pan, heat the olive oil over medium heat. Cook the tofu for 1 minute, then stir in the red onion.

2. Cook for another 2 minutes before adding the turmeric. Add the water and season with soy sauce, kala namak, and black pepper.

3. Cut the tomato into small chunks and add it to the scrambled tofu. Serve.

ALMOND BREAD

SERVES: 15 SLICES

Healthy, gluten free 5 minute sandwich bread. Grain free, and soft. Great for making sandwiches or toasted.

INGREDIENTS

1 cup almond flour

¾ arrowroot flour

½ cup chickpea flour (besan)

⅓ cup coconut oil (solid, not melted)

4 eggs

2 tbsp honey or maple syrup

1 tsp apple cider vinegar

½ tsp sea salt

2 tsp baking powder

METHOD

1. Preheat the oven to 350 degree Fahrenheit. Line a standard bread pan with parchment paper.

2. In a blender, combine all of the ingredients for the bread.

3. Pour the batter into the loaf. Bake at 350 F (180C) for 35 minutes until golden on top.

4. Leave to cool for several minutes before putting out of the pan.

BESAN CHILLA

SERVES: 4

INGREDIENTS

1 cup besan (chickpea flour)

1 medium sized onion, chopped

1 tsp ginger paste

2–3 green chillies, chopped

Handful coriander leaves, chopped

1 tsp turmeric powder

1 tsp red chilli powder

1 cup curd (optional)

Salt as per taste

Oil for pan frying

1 ½ cup water

METHOD

1. Put the besan (chickpea flour) in a bowl.

2. Add onions, green chillies, ginger paste, turmeric powder, red chilli powder, coriander leaves and salt. Mix well.

3. Add water and make a batter. It should be like warm custard consistency.

4. Heat a flat pan. Once hot, add a teaspoon of oil.

5. When the oil is hot, pour in one spoonful of batter and spread it out similar to making an omelette.

6. Add onion, chillies and coriander leaves.

7. Allow it to cook until it is golden in colour and looks cooked.

8. Slowly flip it and cook the other side as well.

9. Remove it from the pan. Serve with curd or chutney.

CHANNA DAL DHOKLA

SERVES: 4

INGREDIENTS

1 cup channa dal (split Bengal gram)

¼ cup yoghurt

1 tsp sugar

FOR THE TEMPERING

1 ½ tbsp. oil

1 tsp mustard seeds

½ tsp red chillies

1/8 tsp asafoetida

1 tbsp water

1 tbsp lemon juice

2 medium green chillies, deseeded sliced lengthwise

2 tbsp coriander leaves, chopped

1 tsp ginger paste

1 tsp turmeric powder

Salt to taste

1 tsp soda

TO GARNISH

Coconut, grated

Coriander leaves, chopped

METHOD

1. Soak the lentils in water for at least 2 hours and blend with the yoghurt, to form the consistency of a pancake batter. Use coconut milk or coconut curd if dairy free.

2. Mix in the sugar and leave in a warm place to ferment overnight.

3. In another bowl mix in the baking soda with oil and leave in a cool place.

4. Mix in the remaining ingredients for the batter after it is fermented.

5. Grease a mould or other suitable vessel and place in a steamer.

6. Add the baking soda to the batter and mix well till light and

fluffy. Immediately pour into the prepared vessel.

7. Cover and steam for 20 minutes.

8. Remove, cool and cut into cubes.

9. Heat oil in a pan and add the mustard seeds; when crackling add the rest of the tempering ingredients.

10. Pour over the dhokla cubes.

13. Garnish by sprinkling grated coconut and coriander leaves.

CHANA SPINACH KEBAB

SERVES: 6

INGREDIENTS

2 cups channa dal

1 cup spinach

¼ cup onion, chopped

¼ cup kasoori methi

1 tsp chopped garlic

1 tsp flax seeds

¼ tsp chopped coriander

1 tsp cumin seeds powder

¼ tsp red chilli powder

¼ tsp saunf powder (fennel seeds powder)

¼ tsp chaat masala

Salt to taste

½ cup poha powder

Oil for frying

METHOD

1. Wash and boil channa dal for 4 to 5 minutes. Dal should not be overly cooked.

2. Wash and chop spinach.

3. Heat oil in a pan, add chopped onion, garlic and chillies and cook until it turns pink in colour.

4. Add chopped palak and cook for 2 to 3 minutes without adding any water.

5. Drain the dal in a sieve and make coarse mixture of dal in a mixer. Add water if required.

6. Add this coarse dal mixture in the spinach pan.

7. Mix well and add all the dry masalas and keep aside for 10 minutes.

8. Make round balls, flatten them, coat with poha flour and fry in oil till golden brown.

FALAFEL

SERVES: 4

INGREDIENTS

1 cup dry chickpeas/garbanzo beans

1 small onion, roughly chopped

¼ cup chopped fresh parsley

3–5 cloves garlic (preferably roasted garlic cloves)

1 ½ tbsp flour or chickpea flour

1 ¾ tsp salt

2 tsp cumin

1 tsp fennel ground

1 tsp ground coriander seeds

¼ tsp black pepper

¼ tsp cayenne pepper

Pinch of ground cardamom

Baking soda (optional)

Vegetable oil for frying

METHOD

1. Pour the chickpeas into a large bowl and cover them up-to about 3 inches of cold water. Let them soak overnight. They will increase in size as they soak – you will have between 4 and 5 cups of beans after soaking.

2. Drain and rinse the garbanzo beans well. Put them into the food processor along with the chopped onion, garlic cloves, parsley, flour or chickpea flour (use chickpea flour to make gluten free), salt, cumin, fennel powder, ground coriander, black pepper, cayenne pepper and cardamom.

3. Pulse all ingredients together until a rough, coarse meal forms. Scrape the sides of the processor periodically and push the mixture down the sides. Process till the mixture is the texture of a thick paste. You want the mixture to hold together, but don't over process, you don't want it turning into hummus!

4. Once the mixture reaches the desired consistency, pour it out into a bowl and use a fork to stir; this will make the texture more even throughout.

5. Some people like to add baking soda to the mixture to lighten up the texture inside of the falafel balls, though the falafel is generally pretty fluffy on its own. If you would like to add it, dissolve 2 tsp of baking soda in 1 tbsp of water and mix it into the falafel mixture after it has been refrigerated.

6. Fill a skillet with vegetable oil to a depth of 1 ½ inches. Heat the oil slowly over medium heat. The ideal temperature to fry falafel is between 360 and 375 degrees F.

7. Meanwhile, form falafel mixture into round balls or slider-shaped patties using wet hands or a falafel scoop. You could

use about 2 tbsp of mixture per falafel. You can make them smaller or larger depending on your personal preference. The balls will stick together loosely at first, but will bind nicely once they begin to fry.

8. If the balls won't hold together, place the mixture back in the processor again and continue processing to make it more paste-like. Keep in mind that the balls will be delicate at first; if you can get them into the hot oil, they will bind together and stick. If they still won't hold together, you can try adding 2–3 tbsp of flour or chickpea flour to the mixture. If they still won't hold, add 1–2 eggs to the mix. This should fix any issues you are having.

9. Before frying the first batch of falafel, you could fry a test one in the center of the pan. If the oil is at the right temperature, it will take 2–3 minutes per side to brown (5–6 minutes total). If it browns faster than that, your oil is too hot and your falafels will not be fully cooked in the center. Cool the oil down slightly and fry again. Serve with pita, hummus and green salad.

HUMMUS

SERVES: 12

INGREDIENTS

2¾ cups of cooked chickpeas, drained

Juice of 1 lemon

5 tbsp oil, preferably extra virgin olive oil

2 tbsp tahini or sesame seed paste

1 clove garlic, crushed

¼ tsp coriander powder

½ tsp cumin powder

½ tsp paprika or ¼ tsp red chilli

1 tsp salt

1 tbsp parsley, finely chopped

TO GARNISH

2 tbsp extra virgin olive oil

½ tsp paprika / sumak

1 tbsp parsley, finely chopped

METHOD

1. Place chickpeas, lemon juice, tahini or sesame seed paste, garlic and coriander and cumin powders in a blender and blend till smooth.

2. Mix in paprika, salt and parsley.

3. Spoon mixture into a serving bowl, drizzle with oil, sprinkle paprika / sumac and parsley. Serve with vegetables sticks, falafel, pita bread.

KHANDVI

SERVES: 4

INGREDIENTS

1 ¼ cups gram flour (chickpea flour)

1 cup yogurt (use coconut curd if dairy free)

1 inch ginger

2 green chillies

4 tablespoons oil

Salt to taste

½ teaspoon turmeric powder

1 tablespoon lemon juice

A pinch of asafoetida

1 tsp mustard seeds

2 tsp coconut, scraped

Few sprigs fresh coriander leaves, chopped

METHOD

1. In a kadhai/wok mix together flour (besan), curd, salt, turmeric, asfoetida and red chilli powder.

2. Add 3 cups water gradually to make a batter.

3. Now turn on the heat (medium flame) and start stirring the batter continuously.

4. Once the batter reaches a thick consistency, turn off the heat.

5. Grease the back side of the plates with a little oil and spread the thickened batter. (Make sure the batter applied is not too thick or the khandvis won't roll.)

6. Let them cool for 10 minutes. Cut strips with a knife and roll.

For the tempering:

In a small pan add oil, mustard seeds, sesame seeds, green chillies and water. Pour over the khandvi.

Garnish with coriander leaves and red chilli powder. Serve hot.

RAM LADDOO MOONG DAL STYLE

SERVES: 6

These high protien balls fried in fresh oil at home are a perfect pair with evening tea.

INGREDIENTS

1 cup moong washed (dhuli) dal

1 cup channa dal

¼ cup chopped spinach

¼ cup grated carrot

¼ cup chopped onion

½ tsp cumin seeds

½ tsp cumin seeds powder

¼ tsp pepper

A pinch of red chilli powder

Salt to taste

Oil for frying

METHOD

1. Wash and soak both dals separately for 4 to 5 minutes.

2. Make fine mixture of the moong dhuli dal and coarse mix of the channa dal.

3. Keep it in the refrigerator for half an hour. Whip well till fluffy.

4. Add chopped vegetables, onions and masalas.

5. Heat oil and fry on medium flame. Serve hot with green chutney.

SPROUTS CHAAT

SERVES: 4

An alkaline high nutrient snack great for breakfast or the devils hour.

INGREDIENTS

1 cup sprouted moong, boiled

¼ cup black gram, sprouted

1 medium onion, finely chopped

1 medium green capsicum, cut into small pieces

1 medium potato, boiled and peeled and chopped into pieces

1 green chilli, finely chopped

2 tbsp lemon juice

Salt to taste

1 tbsp red chilli powder

2 tbsp dried mango powder (amchur powder)

2 tbsp chaat masala

2 tbsp fresh coriander leaves, chopped

2 tbsp sevian (bhujiya) optional

METHOD

1. Mix moong sprouts, black gram (kala chana) sprouts, onion, green capsicum, potato, green chillies, lemon juice, salt, red chilli powder, dried mango powder, chaat masala and coriander leaves in a large bowl.

2. Serve the salad garnished with sevian.

DAL POHA WITH VEGETABLES

SERVES: 4

INGREDIENTS

1 cup moong dal split, soaked for 1 hour

¾ cup mixed vegetables (peas, cauliflower, beans, carrot, capsicum) (boiled/sautéed)

½ cup onion, finely chopped

½ cup tomato, finely chopped

1 green chilli, finely chopped, optional

½ tsp ginger, finely chopped

¼ cup coriander leaves

5–7 curry leaves, finely chopped

A pinch of sugar

½ tsp cooking oil

SPICES

½ tsp black mustard seeds

¼ tsp red chilli powder, optional

¼ tsp turmeric, optional

Salt to taste

METHOD

· Boil vegetables in a small bowl with 1 1/2 cups of water, a pinch of sugar and salt to taste.

· Wash dal and add 2 cups of water and salt to it and boil till done.

· Heat oil in pan, add mustard seeds and allow them to splutter.

· Add ginger and green chilli and cook for about 1 minute.

· Add remaining ingredients including curry leaves and sauté for 2–3 minutes.

· Add dal and vegetables and mix well.

· Add coriander leaves, onion and tomatoes. Serve hot, garnished with curry leaves and chutney.

BLACK CHICKPEAS SUNDAL

SERVES: 4

An excellent filling breakfast dish and snack

INGREDIENTS

1 cup chickpeas

1 red chilli

2 tsp urad dal

2 tsp refined oil

1 pinch asafoetida

1 green chilli

2 pinch salt

2 tsp chana dal

2 tsp coriander seeds

1 tsp mustard seeds

5 leaves curry leaves

FOR GARNISHING

Grated coconut

METHOD

1. To make this delicious snack, soak the black chickpeas in water overnight. Once done, wash, add enough water and pressure cook the black chickpeas for 3-4 whistles. Now heat a pan over moderate flame. Add red chilli, chana dal, urad dal and coriander seeds in the pan and dry fry the ingredients till they turn golden brown. Remove from flame and allow to cool.

2. Now transfer these ingredients in a blender and grind them into a fine powder and keep aside. Heat the pan and add oil in it. Heat it over moderate flame. Add asafoetida, mustard seeds and curry leaves. Once the mustard seeds start to splutter, add the cooked black chickpeas, ground masala powder, green chilli and salt. Mix well.

3. Transfer the scrumptious snack in a serving bowl and garnish with grated coconut and mix well. You can serve this flavourful recipe with a piping hot cup of filter coffee or ginger tea. It is an easy-to-make recipe which can be made in just few minutes, saving on a lot of your time and effort.

KALA CHANA CHAAT

SERVES: 4

Low Glycemic Index snack, keeps you full for long

INGREDIENTS

1 cup dried kala chana/black chickpeas

1 onion

1 tomato

1 green chilli

2 tsp lemon juice

1 tsp coriander leaves, chopped

½ tsp chilli powder

½ tsp chaat masala

½ tsp roasted cumin powder

½ tsp amchur powder

Black salt to taste

METHOD

1. Soak dried chickpeas overnight or for 8–10 hours.

2. Once they are soaked, drain the entire water and pressure cook for 6–7 minutes or 3–4 whistles.

3. Drain the cooked chickpeas.

4. In a large mixing bowl, add all the ingredients along with chickpeas and mix well.

5. Check for the seasoning and add more spice powders and salt if needed.

6. Garnish with some chopped coriander leaves before serving.

MILLET PORRIDGE

SERVES: 4

INGREDIENTS

½ cup Pearl millet whole grains (Bajra) or any other whole millet

1 cup water

1 ½ cups milk / coconut milk / almond milk

½ tsp green cardamom, crushed (optional)

1 tbsp honey or jaggery /2 tbsp fruit purée / date chopped

METHOD

· Boil millet grains in water to cover over moderate heat, till tender. Remove from heat and cool. Alternatively, cook in a pressure cooker with 1 cup of water for 5–7 minutes after cooker reaches full pressure. Open cooker when cool and transfer to a pan.

· Add milk to millet grains and cook over moderate heat to achieve a creamy consistency.

· Stir in cardamom (if used) and honey or jaggery or fruit purée or dates . Serve hot.

VARIATIONS

Replace millet grains with brown rice, sago (sabudana), quinoa or amaranth (ramdana).

MOONG DAL CUTLETS

SERVES: 4

Low Glycemic snack or breakfast

INGREDIENTS

1 cup whole green gram (whole moong dal)

4–5 cups water

1 stick cinnamon

⅛ teaspoon asafoetida

1 tsp oil

½ medium onion, finely chopped

½ tsp cumin seeds

½ tsp dry oregano

2 medium potatoes, boiled

1 whole egg / ¼ cup ground chana

1 tbsp mustard powder

¼ tsp black pepper, freshly ground

Salt or rock salt (black salt) to taste

METHOD

· Combine green gram, water and cinnamon in a pressure cooker, bring to pressure and cook for 25 minutes.

· Heat the oil in a large skillet and add cumin, oregano and onions.

· Sauté until the onion is tender and the herbs are lightly browned.

· Add boiled green gram dal and mash the mixture. Add enough mashed boiled potatoes to bind.

· Stir in the egg white, mustard, salt and pepper to this mixture.

· Add ground chana if the cutlets need binding.

· Form into patties and cook on an iron pan until brown, flipping to brown the other side or cook them in an oven at 350 degree F for 20–30 minutes. Serve the cutlet hot with salad.

Note: These cutlets can be used as a filling for vegetarian burgers.

MOONG DAL IDLI WITH VEGETABLES

SERVES: 4

INGREDIENTS

1 cup moong dal (split green gram)

3 tbsp grated carrot

3 tbsp grated cabbage

1 tbsp ginger-green chilli paste

2 tsp besan (Bengal gram flour)

2 tbsp finely chopped coriander (dhania)

1 tsp ENO

Salt to taste

½ tsp oil for greasing

METHOD

1. Roast the moong dal in a non-stick pan till all the raw smell disappears. Cool and soak in water overnight.

2. Next day, drain and discard the water. Grind the dal in a mixer to a thick paste using little water if required.

3. Add the carrots, cabbage, ginger-green chilli paste, besan, coriander and salt and mix well.

4. Sprinkle the Eno on it and then add few drops of water.

5. When the bubbles form, mix gently.

6. Pour the mixture gently into greased idli moulds and steam in a steamer for 10 to 12 minutes till they are done.

7. Serve hot with coconut chutney.

OATS UPMA

SERVES: 4

INGREDIENTS

1 cup oats

2 tbsp oil

1 tsp urad dal

2 tsp mustard seeds

1 ½ piece ginger, chopped

2 green chillies

8–10 curry leaves

1 chopped medium onion

5–8 chopped French beans

1 medium chopped carrot

¼ cup green peas, fresh or frozen

Salt to taste

½ cup water

METHOD

1. Heat oil.

2. Add urad dal. Once it turns light brown, add mustard seeds.

3. Allow them to crackle.

4. Add ginger, green chillies, curry leaves and onion. Once onion turns light brown, add beans, carrot and peas and mix well.

5. Add salt, and mix well.

6. Cook on low heat till vegetables are cooked.

7. Add oats and mix well. Close lid and cook for 1–2 minutes.

8. Open lid, mix well and serve hot.

PANEER TIKKI

SERVES: 4

INGREDIENTS

200 gms cottage cheese (paneer)

¾ cup shelled green peas, boiled

¾ cup diced carrots, boiled

2 green chillies, chopped A few coriander leaves, chopped

½ tsp garlic paste

1 tsp salt

½ tsp freshly ground black pepper

Oil for shallow-frying

METHOD

1. Mash cottage cheese (paneer) in a bowl.

2. Add remaining ingredients, except oil. Mix well.

3. Divide into 8 portions and shape into flat, round patties.

4. Heat oil in a large frying pan. Grill/ Pan fry tikkis on both sides, in batches if necessary over moderate heat, till cooked and golden brown.

5. Alternatively, place them on a lightly greased baking tray.

6. Bake in an oven preheated to 230°C/450°F/gas mark 8 for 20–25 minutes, turning them around halfway through the baking.

7. Serve hot with coriander chutney.

VARIATION

Use tofu in place of paneer.

QUINOA VEGETABLE PORRIDGE

SERVES: 4

A low-glycemic, high-protein breakfast that keeps you going for long. A great substitute to poha and upma.

INGREDIENTS

2 tsp oil, preferably olive oil

½ tsp cumin seeds (jeera)

½ cup onions, finally chopped

2 cups mixed vegetables, finally chopped (carrot, cabbage, spinach, peas, beans, baby corn, red bell peppers, etc.; choose any four colours)

½ cup quinoa, cooked

Salt to taste

¼ tsp of black pepper

1 tbsp coriander leaves/ parsley, finely chopped

METHOD

1. Heat oil in saucepan. Roast cumin seeds for a few seconds

and add onions. Cook till translucent.

2. Add chopped vegetables and cook for a few minutes.

3. Add quinoa, salt, pepper and 1cup water.

4. Cover the saucepan and cook over low heat for about 15 minutes or until quinoa is done. Alternatively, pressure cook (one whistle).

5. Garnish with fresh coriander or parsley and serve hot.

6. A tangy chutney/relish makes for a great accompaniment.

VARIATION

Quinoa may be substituted with barley or any other whole millet. The tempering may be made with mustard and curry leaves, for a South Indian twist.

SOY TIKKIS

SERVES: 4

INGREDIENTS

100 gms soy granules

1 medium sized potato

5 gms coriander seeds

10 gms ginger paste

10 gms garlic paste

2–3 green chillies

5 gms red chilli powder

20 gms coriander powder

5 gms turmeric power

30 gms green coriander leaves

10 ml Soy refined oil

Soy refined oil for shallow frying

Salt to taste

Seasonal vegetables (1/2 cup) (finely chopped/mashed)

METHOD

1. Soak soy granules in water for 15 minutes. Squeeze in hand to remove excess water.

2. Boil potatoes in salted water, peel and then mash.

3. Wash and chop green chillies.

4. Clean, wash and chop green coriander leaves.

5. Heat oil, add coriander seeds.

6. When it crackles, add ginger paste, garlic paste, green chillies and stir for a moment.

7. Add red chilli powder, coriander powder, turmeric powder while stirring continuously.

8. Add vegetables and soy granules and cook till granules are cooked and dry.

9. Add potato, adjust salt and continue cooking till masala completely dries up.

10. Remove and cool it.

11. Now mix well.

12. Divide into small equal portions and give each portion a cutlet shape.

13. Shallow fry in moderate hot oil until crisp. Serve hot.

SPICY MILLET

SERVES: 4

INGREDIENTS

4 tbsp oil

¼ tsp crushed asafoetida

1 tsp mustard seeds

1 tsp curry powder or garam masala powder

3 cups cooked millet grains (Bajra/Ragi)

1 tsp fresh ginger, chopped/⅛ tsp dried ginger powder (saunth)

1 tsp salt

GARNISH

1 sprig coriander leaves, chopped

METHOD

1. Place oil in a frying pan over moderate heat.

2. When hot, add asafoetida and mustard seeds. After the mustard seeds splutter, add potato and curry powder or garam masala powder.

3. Stir and cook over low heat for 5–7 minutes.

4. Mix in millet, ginger and salt. Remove from heat.

5. Garnish with coriander leaves and serve.

TEEN DAL DOSA

SERVES: 6

INGREDIENTS

⅓ cup parboiled rice

⅓ cup split Bengal gram

⅓ cup split green gram skinless (dhuli moong dal)

2 cups parboiled rice (ukda chawal)

Oil to shallow fry

Pinch of asafoetida

½ tsp cumin seeds

½ tsp melon seeds

2 whole dry red chillies

4–5 curry leaves

2 tsp coconut scraped

½ tsp turmeric powder

Salt to taste

METHOD

· Wash and soak the three dals and rice in six cups of water for four hours. Drain and grind coarsely using a little water.

· Transfer the batter into a deep bowl.

· Heat one tablespoon of oil in a pan and add asafoetida, cumin seeds, mustard seeds, broken dry red chillies and curry leaves. Grind this with coconut into a paste. Add this to the dal batter and mix well. Add turmeric powder and salt and mix well.

· Heat a tava, drizzle some oil, and wipe it with a muslin cloth. Spread a ladleful of batter. Drizzle a little oil all around. Cover and cook on medium heat till the underside is golden.

· Flip over, drizzle some more oil till the other side turns golden. Serve hot.

PAN-FRIED COTTAGE CHEESE WITH CHILLI-GARLIC SAUCE

SERVES: 2

(Protein)

Cottage cheese is immensely filling and adds much-needed calcium to your daily diet. If you tolerate dairy.

INGREDIENTS

3 tsp olive oil

2 tbsp garlic, chopped

1 cup spring onions, chopped

1 tbsp chilli sauce

1 tbsp soy sauce

1 cup cottage cheese, cubed

Salt to taste

White pepper to taste

A pinch of sugar (optional)

METHOD

1. Heat oil over medium flame. Add garlic and spring onions. Cook for about a minute till onions are lightly cooked.

2. Add the rest of the ingredients. Stir-fry for a few minutes till heated through. Serve hot.

LOW CARB PANEER TIKKA

SERVES: 4

Make this low carb quick Paneer Tikka, an Indian cheese, with just a few spices, and pan fry in ghee for a boost of fat to make this keto friendly.

INGREDIENTS

1 ½ cups paneer cut into cubes

2 tsp oil

3-4 cloves garlic minced

2 tsp minced ginger minced

¼ cup cilantro chopped

1 tsp salt

1 tsp garam masala

½ tsp turmeric

½ tsp ground cumin

½ tsp ground coriander

½ tsp smoked paprika for colour and a slightly smoky taste

¼ tsp cayenne pepper

1 tbsp ghee for cooking the paneer

1 lemon juice of 1 lemon for sprinkling before serving

METHOD

1. Place paneer in a bowl and add oil and all the spices. Gently mix everything, taking care to not break the paneer. I found this easiest to do with my hands.

2. Allow this mixture to marinate for about 30 minutes.

3. Heat a skillet, and when it's hot, add two tablespoons of ghee. Lay the paneer cubes in a single layer in the pan.

4. Let it sear for 1-2 minutes, and then using tongs, turn the pieces to sear the other side. Once both sides are seared, you can reduce the heat a little to finish warming the paneer.

5. Spritz the lemon juice right before serving. Paneer tikka can be served as an appetizer or a snack. The cilantro pesto dip would accompany this paneer.

SMOOTHIES AND BEVERAGES

GREEN LEMONADE

SERVES: 1

INGREDIENTS

1 head of romaine lettuce

2 apples, quartered

4 leaves kale

1 lemon

1½ Inch piece ginger

METHOD

1. Process romaine lettuce, apples, kale, lemon and ginger through a juicer.

2. Chill and stir before serving.

CITRUS MARGARITA COOLER

SERVES: 5

INGREDIENTS

1 ½ cup water

½ cup orange juice (fresh preferred)

1 tablespoon lime juice

3 tablespoons of lime juice

METHOD

1. Blend all ingredients except ice in blender until dissolved.

2. Add 4-5 ice cubes and blend on high speed until thickened and smooth.

3. Serve immediately

CHOCOLATE PEANUT BUTTER SMOOTHIE

SERVES: 1

INGREDIENTS

1 large ripe banana (previously peeled, sliced and frozen / 1 large banana equals 200 g)

2 tbsp salted natural peanut butter (if unsalted, add a pinch of salt)

1-2 whole dates (pitted / if not sticky and moist, soak in hot water for 10 minutes, then drain)

1 tbsp cacao powder or unsweetened cocoa powder

1 to 1 ½ cups almond milk

½ cup ice (optional)

ADD-INS OPTIONAL

1 tbsp cacao nibs

1 tbsp flax or hemp seeds(for added nutrition)

Coconut whipped cream for topping

METHOD

1. Add all ingredients except almond milk to the blender.

2. Add in almond milk 1/2 cup at a time, adding only enough to allow the ingredients to blend together. Add more for a thinner shake and less for a thicker shake.

3. Taste and adjust flavours, adding more banana or dates for sweetness, cacao for chocolate flavour, and peanut butter for saltiness.

4. OPTIONAL: Add a handful of ice for extra thickness.

5. Best when fresh, though leftovers will keep in the fridge for up to 24 hours. You could even freeze this into popsicles.

FRUIT SMOOTHIE

SERVES: 1

INGREDIENTS

1 cup (200 ml) yogurt/ almond milk/ coconut milk/ coconut curd

¾ cup seasonal fruit, mashed (banana/ mango/ berries/ papaya / kiwi/ cheeku)

1 tsp honey or date (OPTIONAL)

Crushed ice

METHOD

1. Put yogurt, fruit and honey or date if used in a blender with ice. Blend until smooth.

2. Pour into a tall glass and garnish with fruits.

3. Serve chilled

A teaspoon of (soaked) chia seeds can add to nutrients and taste.

VEGETABLE JUICE

SERVES: 2

INGREDIENTS

200 grams cucumber, peeled and cubed

Lemon juice (optional)

200 grams tomato, medium sized, cut

200 grams carrots, peeled and cubed

500 grams white gourd, peeled and cubed

100 grams beetroot, peeled and cubed

1 bunch celery, chopped

½ bunch spinach

4 amla, deseeded/1 tablespoon lemon juice

1 bunch coriander /mint, broken

1 pinch turmeric (organic)

½ teaspoon black salt

½ teaspoon cumin powder

METHOD

· Run the vegetables except lemon juice (if used) through a juicer/blender

· Season with lemon juice (if used), black salt and cumin powder

· Serve cold garnished with coriander or mint leaves

· Vary it with your own twist and available ingredients

COCONUT MILK CURD

SERVES: 2

INGREDIENTS

1 cup coconut milk

2 tbsp corn starch (dissolved in 2 tbsp water)

1 tsp lemon juice

Probiotic pill optional (lactobacillus)

METHOD

1. Combine coconut milk and corn starches.

2. Cook till thickened like custard.

3. Remove from heat. Add lemon juice and probiotic if used.

4. Refrigerate, it should set like creamy thick curd.

SALAD DRESSINGS

BASIC DRESSING FOR GREENS

SERVES: 2

¼ cup olive oil

2 tbsp balasamic or apple cider vinegar

1 tbsp honey

1 tsp salt

Combine in a cup and blend till smooth and thick.

HEALTHY MAYO

YIELD: 1½ CUPS

INGREDIENTS

2 raw egg yolks, preferably pastured

1 cup quality oil like avocado or light olive oil

2 tbsp fresh lemon juice

1 tbsp water

Sea salt

OR

Egg yolks

Mustard

Lemon juice or apple cider vinegar

Salt and pepper

Olive oil

Coconut oil

METHOD

1. Before you start, make sure all the ingredients are at room temperature.

2. Put the egg yolks in a food processor or blender. Sprinkle with salt and add water.

3. Start blending while slowly pouring the oil into the feed tube.

4. After the mayo has gotten thick, add lemon juice and gently mix with a spoon.

LEMON VINAIGRETTE

YIELD: ⅓ CUP

INGREDIENTS

½ tsp finely grated lemon zest

2 tbsp freshly squeezed lemon juice

1 teaspoon sugar

½ tsp Dijon mustard

¼ tsp fine sea salt, or to taste

3 to 4 tbsp extra-virgin olive oil

Freshly ground black pepper to taste

METHOD

1. In a small bowl, whisk together the lemon zest, lemon juice, sugar, mustard, and fine sea salt, whisking until the sugar and salt are dissolved.

2. Add 3 tbsp of the oil in a slow stream, whisking constantly until the dressing is well blended.

3. Season with fine sea salt and freshly ground black pepper.

4. If desired, whisk in the remaining oil in a slow stream, whisking constantly.

5. The vinaigrette can be prepared ahead and refrigerated, in an airtight container, up to 3 days.

VINAIGRETTE SALAD DRESSING

YIELD: ¼ CUP

INGREDIENTS

3 tbsp extra virgin olive oil (or a more neutral-flavoured oil like grape-seed, canola, or vegetable)

1 tbsp white wine vinegar (or balsamic, apple cider, rice, sherry, or other wine vinegar)

Pinch of kosher salt

A turn of freshly ground black pepper

OPTIONAL ADD-INS

1-2 tbsp fresh chopped herbs like dill, basil, parsley, cilantro, mint, or thyme (dried herbs work, too, just use 1-2 teaspoons instead)

A finely minced garlic clove

2 tsp finely minced or grated ginger

2 tsp finely chopped shallots, scallions, or onion

2 tbsp finely grated or crumbled Parmesan, Pecorino, Romano, Gorgonzola, or Feta

Pinch of crushed red pepper flakes, 1 tablespoon horseradish, or ¼ tsp sriracha

1 tsp Dijon mustard

½ -1 tsp sugar or honey

METHOD

1. Add all of the ingredients to a small mason jar, screw on the lid, and shake until blended. You can also whisk the ingredients together in a bowl or whir them together in a blender.

2. Taste and adjust seasonings if desired. Add to salad, toss, and serve.

3. Keep leftover dressing in a sealed jar in the refrigerator for 2–3 days.

BALSAMIC ALMOND DRESSING

YIELD: ½ CUP

INGREDIENTS

3 tbsp balsamic vinegar

2 tbsp natural almond butter

1 ½ tablespoon pure maple syrup or honey

1 tsp stone ground mustard

1 tsp organic apple cider vinegar (optional)

Salt & pepper to taste

METHOD

1. To make the dressing, add balsamic, almond butter, maple syrup (or honey), mustard, and optional apple cider vinegar, salt/pepper to taste in a small bowl and whisk until combined.

2. You can also mix in jar with lid and shake vigorously, or use a mini food processor.

SALADS

BROCCOLI 'N' SESAME SALAD

SERVES: 2

INGREDIENTS

1 cup broccoli, cut into small florets and steam or cook until still firm

½ cup bell peppers, sliced

1 cup iceberg lettuce or Chinese cabbage, broken

DRESSING

2 tsp light soy sauce

2 tbsp white wine vinegar or lemon juice

2 tsp sesame or peanut oil

1 tbsp honey

1 tbsp sesame seeds, lightly roasted

Salt to taste

White pepper to taste

METHOD

1. Combine ingredients for dressing. Mix well or shake in a bottle till well blended.

2. Combine vegetables and pour dressing.

3. Toss lightly and serve.

PAPAYA BEETROOT SALAD

SERVES: 4

INGREDIENTS

3 cups papaya, cubed

3 cups beetroot, boiled and diced

DRESSING

½ cup vinaigrette

4 tbsp wine vinegar (or other natural vinegar)

2 garlic cloves, minced

6 tsp oil, preferably olive oil

¼ tsp yellow mustard seeds

½ tsp salt

¼ tsp freshly ground pepper

TO GARNISH

Lettuce leaves

METHOD

1. For the vinaigrette, combine all the ingredients in a small bowl. Whisk and blend well. Season with mustard, salt and pepper.

2. Combine papaya and beetroot with the vinaigrette.

3. Toss gently and serve on a bed of lettuce.

FRUIT N NUT COLESLAW SALAD

SERVES: 4

INGREDIENTS

2½ cups shredded cabbage

¾ cup grated carrots

¾ cup dried apricots, deseeded and roughly chopped

½ cup walnuts, roughly chopped

¼ cup seedless raisins (kishmish)

2 tbsp chopped fresh parsley

DRESSING

4 tbsp low-fat mayonnaise

5 tbsp yogurt, whisked smooth

1 ¼ tsp salt

½ tsp black pepper

TO GARNISH

1 apple, sliced

METHOD

1. Combine all salad ingredients in a salad bowl. Toss to mix.

2. In a separate bowl, mix mayonnaise and yogurt and season to taste with salt and pepper.

3. Add mayonnaise to salad and toss till salad is well coated with dressing.

4. Cover bowl and set aside in the refrigerator for at least 30 minutes before serving, to allow the flavours to blend.

5. Serve the coleslaw garnished with apple slices.

INDIAN CHICKPEA SALAD

SERVES - 4

INGREDIENTS

2 cups boiled and drained chickpeas

1 medium red onion (chopped finely)

1 medium tomato (chopped finely)

1 lemon (squeezed - about ¼ cup)

1 cup coriander (finely chopped)

1½ tsp salt

METHOD

1. In a large bowl, add all ingredients and mix until well combined.

2. Refrigerate for at least an hour.

3. When ready to serve, toss the chana salad once more and top with more chopped coriander if desired.

4. Squeeze fresh lemon on the salad.

BURRITO BOWL WITH CAULIFLOWER RICE

SERVES: 4

Cauliflower rice must be organic as far as possible (one of the most heavily pesticides sprayed vegetable)

INGREDIENTS

For Green Chilli Cashew Cream

1 cup raw cashews

¾ cup water

2 tbsp fresh lime juice

2 tbsp canned mild green chillies

⅓ cup coriander

1 garlic clove

¼ teaspoon sea salt

FOR THE BURRITO BOWLS

3 corn tortillas, sliced into strips (tortillas can be substituted with any flat bread or chapatti)

1 recipe seasoned cauliflower rice

2 leeks, white and light green parts, rinsed well and sliced

2 poblano peppers, stem, seeds and ribs removed, thinly sliced (mild chilli peppers)

1 garlic clove, minced

½ tsp dried oregano

1 cup cooked black beans, drained and rinsed

2 ripe mangoes, cubed

1 avocado, diced

½ cup chopped cilantro

Lime wedges, for serving

Extra-virgin olive oil
Sea salt and freshly ground black pepper

METHOD

1. Make the cashew cream. In a blender, combine the cashews, water, lime juice, green chillies, cilantro, garlic, and salt. Blend until creamy.

2. Make the burrito bowls. Preheat the oven to 350°F and line a baking sheet with parchment paper. Place the tortilla strips on the baking sheet and toss with a drizzle of olive oil and a pinch of salt. Bake for 10 minutes or until crispy. Remove from the oven and set aside.

3. In a medium skillet, heat 1 teaspoon of olive oil over medium heat. Sauté the leeks and poblanos with generous pinches of salt and pepper. Cook until soft for 7 to 10 minutes, and then add the minced garlic and oregano. Stir, cook for 1 minute, then add a squeeze of lime and remove from heat.

4. Assemble the burrito bowls with the cauliflower rice, poblano mixture, black beans, mango, avocado, and cilantro. Drizzle with the cashew cream and top with the crispy tortilla strips. Serve with lime wedges and additional cashew cream.

A high-powered blender is best for this, otherwise, soak your cashews for 2 hours or overnight and drain before using.

How to make Cauliflower Rice?

There are two techniques for making cauliflower rice. You can either use a box grater with the medium-size holes traditionally used for cheese, or a food processor with the grater blade to blitz it into small pieces. With both techniques you're aiming for little pieces the size of rice.

Press any excess moisture from the rice by transferring the cauliflower rice to a large paper towel or absorbent dish towel and squeeze/press to remove any remaining water. This ensures no excess moisture remains, which can make your dish soggy.

Once you have your cauliflower rice, it's easy to cook! Simply sauté in a large skillet over medium heat in 1 tbsp oil. Use a lid to cover so the cauliflower stems become more tender. Cook for a total of 5-8 minutes, stirring occasionally, then season as desired (such as with soy sauce or salt and pepper).

ROASTED SWEET POTATOES

SERVES: 6

INGREDIENTS

4 cups (1 kg) sweet potatoes, cut into 2-inch pieces

2 tbsp olive oil or canola oil

1 tsp salt

¾ tsp freshly ground black pepper

2 tbsp finely chopped garlic (8 cloves garlic)

2 tbsp fresh chopped parsley

METHOD

1. Preheat the oven to 220°C | 425°F. Lightly spray a baking sheet or tray with cooking oil spray.

2. Arrange the sweet potatoes on the sheet in one layer, and add the oil, salt, pepper, and garlic. Toss until the potatoes are well coated and seasoned.

3. Roast in the oven for 45 -55 minutes, while flipping occasionally, until tender.

4. Remove the sweet potatoes from the oven and season with a little extra salt and pepper to taste. Sprinkle over with parsley and serve immediately!

Not suitable for storing.

FARRO SALAD

SERVES: 6

INGREDIENTS

1 cup whole-grain farro (can be substituted with millets or brown rice or quinoa)

2 cups vegetable broth

1 ½ tsp salt

1 bay leaf

1 large shallot, very thinly sliced

1/3 cup extra virgin olive oil

3 tbsp apple cider vinegar

1 tbsp dijon mustard

2 tsp honey

Freshly ground black pepper

2 cup lightly packed arugula

1 green apple, chopped

½ cup shaved parmesan cheese

¼ cup freshly chopped basil

⅛ cup freshly chopped parsley

¼ cup toasted pecans, roughly chopped

THE DRESSING

Few things are more delicious than fried shallots. They're packed with flavour, and add a much-needed crunch to your grain salad. Not only that, but they infuse the oil that's used for the dressing! That infused shallot oil teams up with apple cider vinegar, dijon mustard, and honey to create a super flavourful dressing we can put on literally anything.

1. THE FARRO

Sure, boiling farro in water is fine. But boiling farro in broth is SO much more flavorful. We like adding a bay leaf too, and feel free to add your favourite hearty herbs like rosemary or thyme.

2. THE MIX-INS

With nuts, cheese, fruit, and leafy greens, this salad really feels like a full meal—aka a meal prepper's dream. It makes the perfect not-so-sad desk lunch. Top it with some sliced grilled or smoked chicken or baked salmon and you've got yourself a very hearty, very healthy meal.

3. THE VERSATILITY

Not a fan of pecans? Use walnuts instead. You could use pears and ditch the apples too. This salad is a sort of template for a good grain salad. It's got all the elements you need: sweet, salty, soft, crunchy, fatty, fresh. Feel free to make it your own with your preferred mix-ins.

METHOD

1. In a medium saucepan, combine farro, vegetable broth, salt and bay leaf. Bring to a boil, then reduce to a simmer and let cook, stirring occasionally, until farro is tender and no broth remains (for about 30 minutes). When farro is cooked, transfer to a large bowl to cool.

2. In the meantime, make fried shallots: in a small saucepan over medium heat, combine oil and shallots. When the shallots begin to bubble, reduce heat to medium-low and cook, stirring

occasionally, until shallots are golden and crisp, for about 15 to 20 minutes. Remove shallots from oil with a slotted spoon and place on a paper-towel lined plate and season with salt. Let oil cool.

3. Make dressing: in a medium bowl, combine the cooled olive oil with vinegar, mustard and honey; and season with salt and pepper.

4. Assemble salad: combine cooked farro, crispy shallots, arugula, apple, parmesan, basil, parsley and pecans. Drizzle dressing over salad and toss to coat.

SOUPS

CHICKEN SOUP

SERVES: 4

INGREDIENTS

1 small (400 gm) chicken (include all scraps and bones)

½ tsp ginger (grated)

1 tsp garlic (crushed)

1 large onion (finely chopped)

1 stick cinnamon

4-5 cloves

2 bay leaves

½ tsp dried rosemary

3 cups water

½ tsp black pepper (optional)

Salt to taste

METHOD

1. Put all the above ingredients into a pressure cooker and

cook for 2-3 whistles.

2. When cool, strain the soup. Discard the solids. Debone the chicken and shred the meat. Add to the soup.

3. Adjust seasoning and serve hot.

MUSHROOM SOUP

SERVES: 2

INGREDIENTS

½ cup mushrooms (washed and grated)

1 tsp butter

¼ tsp dried rosemary

¾ cup water

Salt to taste

METHOD

1. Heat butter and add mushrooms and rosemary. Sauté for 5 minutes.

2. Add water and bring to gentle simmer. Simmer for 2-3 minutes.

3. Cool slightly and then add salt to taste. Serve hot.

TOMATO BASIL SOUP

SERVES: 4

INGREDIENTS

6 medium tomatoes

1 large carrot (chopped)

2 medium onions (chopped)

½ tsp garlic (crushed)

½ cup fresh basil leaves

2 cups water

1 tbsp olive oil

Salt to taste

METHOD

1. Cut tomatoes in half. Place in baking tray, skin side down. Drizzle with olive oil and salt and place in hot oven (220 degrees) until skin is wrinkled and beginning to char. Remove and cool.

2. Peel skin. Place tomatoes, carrot, onions, garlic, salt and water in a pressure cooker and cook for 2 whistles.

3. When cool, blend the soup and strain it.

4. Reheat and add finely chopped basil.

5. Adjust seasoning, serve hot.

SPINACH SOUP

SERVES: 2

INGREDIENTS

1 cup spinach (blanched and pureed)

1 tsp butter or olive oil

¼ onion (finely chopped)

½ tsp ginger juice

1 tsp cornflour

Salt to taste

Ground black pepper (optional)

METHOD

1.Heat butter gently and add the onion. Sautee until translucent.

2. Add pureed spinach and ginger juice and stir.

3. Whisk cornflour in water and add to saucepan.

4. Keep stirring on gentle heat until soup starts simmering.

Let simmer for 2-3 minutes.

5. Cool slightly and add salt to taste. Serve hot.

VEGETARIAN MAINS

LEMON RICE

SERVES: 4

INGREDIENTS

½ cup skinned peanuts

1 tsp salt

2 cups long-grained rice cooked

¼ cup lemon juice

TEMPERING

2 tbsp oil

2 tsp mustard seeds

2 tsp husked split Bengal gram (chana dal)

1 tsp husked split black gram (urad dal)

10–12 curry leaves

4 green chillies, seeded and chopped

1 tsp turmeric powder

GARNISH

2 tbsp toasted sesame seeds (til), optional

1–2 sprigs curry leaves

METHOD

1. Place oil for tempering in a pan over moderate heat. When hot, add mustard seeds and allow them to splutter. Add remaining tempering ingredients and fry till dals are golden.

2. Add peanuts and stir gently, till light golden. Stir till the rice is well-coated with spices.

3. Garnish with sesame seeds (if used) and curry leaves.

4. Serve hot with rasam or raita.

VEGETABLE FRIED RICE

SERVES: 4

INGREDIENTS

1 cup extra-firm tofu* (8 ounces yields ~1 cup)

1 cup long- or short-grain brown rice* (rinsed thoroughly in a fine mesh strainer)

4 cloves garlic (minced)

1 cup chopped green onion

½ cup peas

½ cup carrots (finely diced)

SAUCE

3 tbsp tamari or soy sauce (plus more for veggies + to taste)

1 tbsp peanut butter.

2-3 tbsp organic brown sugar, muscovado sugar, or maple syrup

1 clove garlic (minced)

1-2 tsp chilli garlic sauce

1 tsp toasted sesame oil (optional / or sub peanut or avocado oil)

METHOD

1. Preheat oven to 400°F (204° C) and line a baking sheet with parchment paper (or lightly grease with non-stick spray).

2. In the meantime wrap tofu in a clean, absorbent towel and set something heavy on top (such as a cast iron skillet) to press out the liquid.

3. Once the oven is preheated, dice tofu into ¼ inch cubes

and arrange on baking sheet. Bake for 26-30 minutes. You're looking for golden brown edges and a texture that's firm to the touch. The longer it bakes, the firmer and crispier it will become, so if you're looking for softer tofu remove from the oven around the 26-28 minute mark. I prefer crispy tofu, so I bake mine the full 30 minutes. Set aside.

4. While the tofu bakes prepare your rice by bringing 2 cups of water to a boil in a large pot. Once boiling, add rinsed rice and stir. Boil on high uncovered for 30 minutes, then strain for 10 seconds and return to pot removed from the heat. Cover with a lid and let steam for 10 minutes*.

5. While rice and tofu are cooking, prepare sauce by adding all ingredients to a medium-size mixing bowl and whisking to combine. Taste and adjust flavour as needed, adding more tamari or soy for saltiness, peanut butter for creaminess, brown sugar for sweetness, or chilli garlic sauce for heat.

6. Once the tofu is done baking, add directly to the sauce and marinate for 5 minutes, stirring occasionally.

7. Heat a large metal or cast iron skillet over medium heat. Once hot, use a slotted spoon to scoop the tofu into the pan leaving most of the sauce behind. Cook for 3-4 minutes, stirring occasionally, until deep golden brown on all sides. Lower heat if browning too quickly. Remove from pan and set aside.

8. To the still hot pan add garlic, green onion, peas and carrots. Sauté for 3-4 minutes, stirring occasionally, and season with 1 tbsp (15 ml) tamari or soy sauce.

9. Add cooked rice, tofu, and remaining sauce and stir. Cook over medium-high heat for 3-4 minutes, stirring frequently.

10. Serve immediately with extra chilli garlic sauce or sriracha for heat (optional). Crushed salted, roasted peanuts or cashews make a lovely additional garnish. Leftovers keep well in the refrigerator for 3-4 days, though best when fresh. Reheat in a skillet over medium heat or in the microwave.

Notes

*If you don't like tofu, you can sub 1 cup fresh mushrooms – add in with vegetables.

*For the rice, you can also substitute a comparable amount of quinoa.

*Nutrition information is a rough estimate.

BUDDHA BOWL

SERVES: 4

INGREDIENTS

RICE AND VEGGIES

1 ¼ cups short grain brown rice or long-grain brown rice, rinsed

1 ½ cups frozen shelled edamame, preferably organic

1 ½ cups trimmed and roughly chopped snap peas or snow peas, or thinly sliced broccoli florets

1 to 2 tbsp reduced-sodium tamari or soy sauce, to taste

4 cups chopped red cabbage or spinach or romaine lettuce or kale (ribs removed)

2 ripe avocados, halved, pitted and thinly sliced into long strips (wait to slice just before serving)

ESSENTIAL GARNISHES

1 small cucumber, very thinly sliced

Dressing of your choice.

Thinly sliced green onion (about ½ small bunch)

Lime wedges

Toasted sesame oil, for drizzling

Sesame seeds

METHOD

1. Bring a large pot of water to boil (ideally about 4 quarts water). Once the water is boiling, add the rice and continue boiling for 25 minutes. Add the edamame and cook for 3 more minutes (it's okay if the water doesn't reach a rapid boil again). Then add the snap peas and cook for 2 more minutes.

2. Drain well, and return the rice and veggies to the pot. Season to taste with 1 to 2 tablespoons of tamari or soy sauce, and stir to combine.

3. Divide the rice/veggie mixture and raw veggies into 4 bowls. Arrange cucumber slices along the edge of the bowl. Drizzle lightly with carrot ginger dressing and top with sliced green onion. Place a lime wedge or 2 in each bowl.

4. When you're ready to serve, divide the avocado into the bowls. Lightly drizzle sesame oil over the avocado, followed by a generous sprinkle of sesame seeds and flaky sea salt. Serve promptly.

5. If you intend to have leftovers, wait to complete step 4 just before serving (otherwise the avocado will brown too soon). Leftover bowls keep well (avocado excluded) for 4 to 5 days in the refrigerator.

NOTES

CARROT GINGER DRESSING NOTE: You're probably only going to need ½ batch of the dressing for 4 bowls. I recommend making the full batch since blenders require a decent volume of liquid to blend. Just use the leftover dressing on salads within 1 to 2 weeks of making.

MAKE IT QUICK: If you're in a hurry, you can skip the dressing and drizzle tamari and toasted sesame oil lightly over the bowls instead.

MAKE IT VEGAN: Be sure to follow the vegan option while making the carrot-ginger dressing.

MAKE IT GLUTEN FREE: Be sure to use certified gluten-free tamari, instead of soy sauce. Or, omit the soy sauce altogether and season the rice with salt, to taste.

MAKE IT SOY FREE: Omit the tamari/soy sauce and season the rice with salt, to taste.

NON-VEGETARIAN MAINS

CHICKEN WITH PEANUT BUTTER

SERVES: 2

INGREDIENTS

1 chicken breast

1 tbsp coconut oil

1 onion – chopped

2 cloves of garlic – chopped

¼ tsp of chilli powder

2 tbsp peanut butter

Bunch of parsley or coriander

2 cups potato / sweet potato / pumpkin

1 tsp of salt

¼ cup of coconut milk

METHOD

1. Rub the chicken with salt.

2. In a frying pan melt the coconut oil and fry the chicken breast until golden on both sides. Then cover it with a lid to steam the chicken breast on a low heat.

3. When chicken is cooked through, add chopped onion, garlic and chilli, cover and steam for about 5 minutes occasionally

stirring.

4. Take the chicken out of the pan and to the sauce add peanut butter and stir until smooth.

POTATOES

1. Peel the potatoes or pumpkin and cube it, boil it until soft.

2. Drain the water and add the salt, coconut milk and mash it. Serve with greens of your choice.

WRAPS

ASIAN CHICKEN LETTUCE WRAPS

SERVES: 4

INGREDIENTS

3 tbsp hoisin sauce

2 tbsp low-sodium soy sauce

2 tbsp rice wine vinegar

1 tbsp Sriracha (optional)

1 tsp sesame oil

1 tbsp extra-virgin olive oil

1 medium onion, diced

2 cloves garlic, minced

1 tbsp freshly grated ginger

2½ cups ground chicken

½ cup water chestnuts, drained and sliced

2 green onions, thinly sliced

Salt to taste

Freshly ground black pepper

Large leafy lettuce (leaves separated), for serving

Cooked white rice, for serving (optional)

METHOD

1. Make the sauce: In a small bowl, whisk together hoisin sauce, soy sauce, rice wine vinegar, Sriracha, and sesame oil.

2. In a large skillet over medium-high heat, heat olive oil. Add onions and cook until soft, 5 minutes, then stir in garlic and ginger and cook until fragrant, 1 minute more. Add ground chicken and cook until opaque and mostly cooked through, breaking up meat with a wooden spoon.

3. Pour in sauce and cook 1 to 2 minutes more, until sauce reduces slightly and chicken is cooked through completely. Turn off heat and stir in chestnuts and green onions. Season with salt and pepper.

4. Spoon rice, if using, and a large scoop (about 1/4 cup) of chicken mixture into the centre of each lettuce leaf. Serve immediately.

COLLARD WRAP BENTO BOXES

SERVES: 4

INGREDIENTS

4 tbsp hummus

1 medium cucumber, peeled and sliced into matchsticks

2 medium carrots, peeled and sliced into matchsticks

1 cup shredded purple cabbage

2 avocados, pitted and sliced

½ cup shredded chicken or sautéed tofu

4 large collard leaves, ribs removed

FOR EACH BENTO BOX

1 cup mixed carrot and celery sticks

½ cup grapes or berries

¼ cup 70% dark chocolate

METHOD

1. Spread 1 tablespoon hummus in the middle of each collard leaf. Divide veggies and chicken or tofu among the leaves and gently roll each up into a wrap.

2. Halve each wrap and serve with bento box additions.

DESSERTS

FLOUR-LESS GRIDDLE CAKE

SERVES: 1

Quick, easy and high on nutrition.

INGREDIENTS

1 banana

2 eggs

Pinch of salt

Olive / coconut oil for pan frying

Vanilla – optional

METHOD

1. Mash the banana until smooth.

2. Add eggs and salt and whisk it together.

3. Heat up iron griddle with some olive/ coconut oil.

4. Pour the batter on the griddle and cover it with a lid, to cook well.

5. Flip the cake over and cook again for a few minutes.

6. Serve hot / cold with honey/ berries/ maple syrup.

CHIA SEEDS PUDDING

SERVES: 2

Rich in fibre and anti-inflammatory omega-3 fats. This dessert should not make you feel guilty.

INGREDIENTS

1 cup of coconut or other nut milk

4 tbsp of chia seeds

1 cup papaya, cubed finely (reserve a few to decorate)

1 cup pineapple cubed finely (reserve a few to decorate)

METHOD

1. Put 2 tbsp of chia seeds in two tall glasses.

2. Add half a cup of nut milk to each glass and stir regularly to avoid clumping. When you see that the mixture is getting thicker, you can stir it less and eventually leave it out or in the fridge for 10 minutes to set.

3. Coarsely puree the fruit.

4. Pour the fruit onto the chia pudding.

5. Decorate the glass with some cubes and serve.

BEST CHOCOLATE CAKE

SERVES: 12

This flour-less chocolate cake could not get healthier and richer!

INGREDIENTS

2 cups raw sweet potato minced

2 large eggs

¾ cup cocoa powder

½ cup coconut oil

½ cup honey

½ cup coconut sugar

¼ cup coconut flour

1 tbsp almond or vanilla extract

2 tsp baking powder

1 tsp salt

FROSTING

1 ¾ cup sweet potato cubed and boiled

½ cup avocado or cashew paste

½ cup soft medjool dates

½ cup cocoa powder

1 tsp almond or vanilla extract

¼ tsp sea salt

METHOD

1. Preheat the oven to 180°C. Line the bottom of one medium round cake form with parchment paper.

2. In a food processor mince sweet potato. Then in a blender combine all ingredients for cake until smooth.

3. Pour the batter in a medium size round cake form. Bake on 180°C for 45-50 minutes then chill in the freezer while you are making the frosting.

4. Cooled boiled potatoes blend with the rest of ingredients until smooth and chill until ready to frost.

OPTIONAL TOPPINGS: chocolate chips or chocolate glaze and berries.

CHOCOLATE GLAZE: In a double boiler over medium heat melt ¼ cup coconut oil, ¼ cup cocoa powder and 2 tbsp honey. Once melted remove from heat, cool, pour over cake.

Food Habits in Corporate Offices

A first-hand experience contributed by, Mr. Devendra Bhatnagar, Managing Director, Wholefoods India.

Food habits across the nation for office goers reflects the changing socio structure of family and location. With both partners working, home cooked food by and large is limited to possibly one meal a day or on weekends. In the younger generation either they are living apart from their parents or are located in a city remote from their hometown. This leads to them eating all their meals from a third party source.

What we eat definitely defines us. Given the fact that on an average most office goers spend 9-10 hours at the workplace and two hours on transit time to and fro, they end up eating two main meals outside and/or one main meal and two snacks

Studies show that businesses suffer due to downtime from unhealthy employees both in insurance costs and also non-productivity. Stemming from this fact alone corporates worldwide have incorporated studies, committees and taken steps to introduce certain directives to their in-house food committees on food safety and food monitoring services.

Here are those criterion, their objectives and downsides:

• Breakout areas to be provided for social interaction and accessibility to coffee/tea vending machines and cookies-biscuits.

• A dining room or cafeteria space to be provided with

space permitting multiple food options.

• Food options should have a section earmarked 'healthy options'.

• Food safety and practices at the dispensing end be monitored by an in-house F&B team.

• Food committees to meet regularly with vendors to set the menu/pricing/give feedback/address complaints if any.

• Corporate policy permitting, food served could either be subsidized by the company in addition to vendor discounts in lieu of space rentals with waiver of electricity charges or the employee pays for food without subsidies but at discounts offered by the vendor.

• That the price points are kept low keeping in account the salary status mix of employees in the workplace.

In terms of stated policies most progressive international MNC corporates do have a clearly stated Food Safety & Services policy in place which is evident in the workplace as well as for the service providers. But for most other offices the quest for getting the right vendor, with hygienic manufacturing setup, system and processes, adherence to HACCP / FSMS and associated compliances on a practical level are on paper but not always executed.

Healthy Workplace is a buzzword that encompasses

ergonomics of work desk, seating, ambience, amenities, working conditions and food. If a person is confined to longish hours with not much physical activity, one needs to have the right intake both in terms of food and beverages. Modern lifestyle-related diseases are directly linked to this sedentary lifestyle coupled with overly processed fast foods and beverages rich in oil, sugars, salts and preservatives, as the case may be.

All good till now. But let's look at the practical implementation at ground level and where the twist in the tale lies.

For a start, the premixed cheap tea/coffee machines at the breakout stations are a direct source of sugar that goes into stabilizing the premixed dried milk powder. And during the course of a day an average employee would consume 5 cups. The coffee machine's internal piping /components need cleaning and flushing at least twice a day. This is normally neglected.

In the present day, realty spaces are very expensive and most offices limit the recreation-cafeteria spaces to the minimum size possible. This acts as a deterrent for many of their employees from either visiting the cafeteria during meal times when they either grab a meal on the go (read: fast food processed snacks) and/or phone in deliveries for food to be consumed at their desk or breakout areas.

Then there is the question of self-induced or work-related stress where too the employees trade good honest food which may take time to be served and consumed for the quick alternative of fast foods which unfortunately are the principle cause of most ills.

Choices we make dictate how we live our lives and become the foundation of how life in all its dimensions play out. Choice of food therefore assumes significance of the highest order. The keywords being choices on offer, personal commitment, knowledge and awareness. In the progressive corporates we arguably look up to their wisdom in addressing all good practices but for most the easier path is in the statement – we are talking of adults aren't we?

So on the subject of choices, we find that coffee shops and fast food kiosks, swank in their ambience, efficient in space and attractive marketing, occupies centre stage followed by local operators with absolutely tasty but heavy on creams, oils, sugar and salt, besides no balancing of nutritive requirements. An operator dealing in health foods, space permitting, then gets last preference. So in effect the healthier option even today remains a step sister or an afterthought and definitely the last option.

The culture of having an independent wing of monitoring food services within the facility management is incorporated in most multinational companies of good international repute and size. For others the facility manager or the HR manager serves the role. Having an independent cell or vertical ensures a 24 x 7 oversight which as a food manufacturer I may find intrusive but in the larger picture a very welcome component leading to increased efficiency, hygiene and quality of food and food services.

Nearly 99% of institutions and corporates make one initial visit to the food vendor's manufacturing unit where they verify the licenses, the compliances and the facility itself. Primary objective being to avoid a national or international fallout in case of any lapses in the future. After the incorporation of the vendor as a food supplier or operator to their office the verification is limited to random food tasting at the office only.

Herein lies a major lapse. The food manufacturer/supplier for the preliminary visit presents his/her commissary in the best possible light but in the subsequent intervening months or years due to various bottom line factors they may have compromised on their upkeep, quality of staff or even quality of raw material.

Some corporations (less than a percent) audit the facility(s) of their food service provider each month by engaging an external agency qualified to do so. The audits on the lines of ISO qualifications monitor FSMS/HACCP/SOP/Hygiene/Infrastructure maintenance of the service provider. This is a very laudable approach and more so as it comes at a fiscal cost to the organization. But it is worth every cent as it ensures an all-around upgradation, learning, conformity and therefore the final service is as 'safe' as is humanly possible.

It would be ideal if all corporations took such a progressive outlook. I know as a manufacturer how this continuous scrutiny of how we run our facility has added to our reputation in the market. And this is only due to the vision of one corporation of the many such and healthcare institutions we serve.

I appreciate but do not support the view taken by all under the umbrella statement – that's anyway the quality we expect from a professional outfit and we are not equipped to be the class monitor outside our territory!

A necessary progression within most corporates is to have a food committee as a one point of direct interaction to food services, food quality and prices within the office space as contracted to serve in, by the vendor. The committee consists of representatives from the corporation's employees, management, facility managers and the procurement team of the management. They also serve as a grievance cell for any employee complaint with respect to the food. Even though the minutest observation is escalated up the chain, this serves as a professional pressure point on the service provider to be always on their toes. Initially this can be stressful but, along the way like in all 'learnings', the basic observations reduce, indicating that the vendor is incorporating better practices.

Very few corporations subsidize the food directly or offer free meals. They negotiate better and lower rates from the vendors by not charging any rentals and/or waive electricity charges and facility upkeep charges in keeping with their stated CSR in-house policies.

Here lie the genesis of most problems. Within any office space the employee salary brackets vary sharply with the ranks. Therefore the prices of food being served comes at near rock bottom and with competition even the quality of raw materials purchased is compromised.

Food should not alone be merited on taste alone but on the ingredients and on the nutritive quality the processed (finished) product offers. Each meal should be tailored for the consumer and their needs to fulfill the very basic criteria of 'well-being' that food must offer.

By and large food options in corporations vary from country

to country, space availability, number of employees within a branch office and accessibility to phone-call-in-delivery. Also it is a direct result of food habits with a heavy influence of local specialties prevalent. Certain fast foods have crossed continents and can be found everywhere.

Within the most progressive of organizations there is always a health committee which may or may not be separate from the food committee. It is normally headed by a Vice President level management personnel to bring focus to its seriousness of intent. Its charter is well-being of the employee through awareness programmes, access to validated food, physical checkups, physical activities and prominent noticeboards that recognize personal achievement in the all-encompassing category of 'well-being and achievements within same space'.

Having discussed at length the steps taken by the corporates and institutions to tie up with food vendors, it is time to look at the vendors' story in this association.

There is always excitement at the prospect of opening a food space in a corporate office. The clientele and its numbers are known. They don't vary. Of course if the work force is larger, multiple vendors often service the food courts. One has to understand that with captive audiences the level of boredom from 'set' menus can be pretty quick. So multiple cuisines and the flexibility to adapt to a new menu or incorporation of new dishes is de rigueur. Take a country of the size and diversity of India with a varied cuisine from 5 zones, including central India. Each zone has its own street food, main cuisines and desserts. Besides this, the fast foods from the West and from China, prepared the Indian way.

The office space itself has a diverse mix of employees, many of whom are away from home and desirous of a taste of their 'home'. For the vendor, competition may be a sharing of revenues (myopic view) but if monitored well it brings vibrancy to the cafeteria space. Monitored well – I use that term to explain an often found conundrum which is that nearly all the vendors end up serving a similar fare. This is the modern day corporate version of the high street restaurant billboards: Indian-Mughlai-Chinese-Continental. Wonderful, except it's all on one billboard, in one kiosk. It does not rob one of imagination but definitely of quality and 'quality for money'. Here the food committee can be progressive in monitoring that each vendor has a focused menu and has the requisite expertise in the same. So instead of being a diverse food court in most places it becomes repetitive food offerings. Understandably, the staff in their limited break time are looking for minimum time wasted in ordering /consuming food/waiting in queues and then having gulped (gorged is a wrong term) ready-to-eat fast foods. They proceed for a cigarette and/or to talk/gossip with friends before heading back to their work station. Therefore, despite an opportunity to order minimally processed foods that may take 5 or 10 minutes to prepare/assemble and serve, averagely the hand reaches out for what is ready to eat.

There is a concept of 'coolness' associated for Indians with pizzas, risottos, pies, pasta, burger, lasagna, fries, oversized burgers, noodles, fried Manchurian rice, garlic bread, packed sandwiches with processed fillings, etc. Thanks to marketing, exposure to Hollywood and American TV. And then there are the Indian fast foods – mostly deep fried, coated in flour and batter – samosas, bread pakoras, bhajia, puff pastry, etc.

Some people know that you are what you eat. But with the availability of these options they would much rather let someone else do the thinking and planning instead of making educated choices which are available if one has the patience. It is not that all fast foods are unhealthy for we have some good and healthy fare from all corners of the earth, including India. So it is the association between comfort food and stress at work that makes one go for that unhealthy choice. Also often:

• One doesn't have the time to head out and get lunch.

Times have changed with regard to perception of what is 'qualitative eating' time.

• Grab & Go sounds classy and makes one look busy
• To eat on the fly matches one's mind and personality
• The other fare on offer is insipid
• One does not know what is healthy

In all fairness most of us are at all times easily tempted by any finger food especially 'junk food' for we look at its portion and assume it to be lesser fare than our normal home food and therefore assume it has less calories etc. However, the more the food (especially junk food) is processed, the more harmful it is because it is loaded in some form or the other with premixes/preservatives/hydrogenated fat/salt or sugar besides artificial flavours/colours etc. Most 'junk foods' of a particular brand are processed and manufactured by their outsourced dedicated unit located in one or two cities and supplied under cold chain management across the country to hundreds of their franchised outlets. From the point of standardization this is the perfect solution but from the point of view of health it is disastrous.

When does this take its toll? Stands to reason if one is habituated to eating out, has access to fast food and does not have awareness of what constitutes unhealthy food or less nutritive food then one is destined to various lifestyle related problems, some immediate and some later on in life.

India boasts of rampant diabetes, both adult and juvenile, has a high cancer rate and exceptionally high cardiovascular problems. Our lifestyle and habits don't help us any. And the problem is only increasing.

The old saying – one is what one eats – remains true despite all the marketing blitz that food processing and fast food companies put forward. But can we fool all the people all the time? And this despite their so-called awareness and education. I am not a medical person trained in cellular behaviour where neurons, receptors and dopamine play character roles in our decisions. But as a food operator of conscience where my company, Whole Foods India has clearly defined the vision, goals and the path to tread and reached the goals that it wished to, irrespective of profits/losses or as the trade jargon is, bottom line. We've also had the opportunity to observe the human frailties when it comes to decision-making regarding food.

Conscious nutritionists, researchers and practicing doctors are continuously battling against an "industry" that is leading the consumers down a path not conducive to good health. And what is good health? They help us understand that back-to-basics is what this is all about. With the help of science, knowledge and scientific quest we can understand the intake of nutrients, fats, sugars and salt that is required and predict and direct the course we should undertake physically. Today these trained eyes and minds are studying how, besides the physical aspect, the mind too reacts to food.

Let's approach 'stress' as we are discussing the environment in corporate offices. Studies have shown that these have far-reaching consequences and broadly fall into:.

- Self inflicted due to inadequacy
- Self inflicted due to delivery of results/pressure
- Self inflicted due to unrealistic goals/aspirations
- Office inflicted due to the culture of expectations
- Office related due to competition
- Office related due to unrealistic time frames/pressure.

The young employee is submerged under a huge stress induced work pattern that leads them to apportion minimum time for their own well-being and sleep.

Here steps in "food". Good old fashioned, mom's cooking, wholesome, tasty, warm and nutritious because it is simply fresh. Certain foods help overcome erratic behaviour, then there are foods that help one calm down, and quell the turmoil within. But then also there are foods that inflame the stress levels, transposed chemically or from their own trauma. One of the latest studies relates how animals before slaughter, sensing their end, are stressed and traumatized. This in turn is passed on to the meat which we consume. This is not a diatribe against "meats" but just to explore that there is more to food than just gulping it down.

All corporate offices must provide access to simple, quality, minimally processed foods that are intelligently constructed, portioned for a sedentary lifestyle, balanced in the body's nutrition requirement and lists the calorie content. They must insist on food with a short shelf life.

Topping the list of food consumables in India, after deep fried savouries, followed by desserts (sweets), in third place stands "cooking oil". Surely that's a recipe for disaster. It is. And it wears the same mask – food is being indiscriminately served and equally foolishly consumed.

READ MORE

ALKALINE WATER

While most health seekers are on cleansing diets, hitting the gym, practicing yoga, purifying air through filters, water quality has not been high on the agenda.

It seems the time to address water quality beyond microbial purity has come.

Human body requires a tightly controlled pH level in the serum of about 7.4 (a slightly alkaline range of 7.35 to 7.45) to survive.

There is emerging evidence to suggest that the PH of water has a strong correlation with the functioning of our body and prevention of diseases.

Alkaline water has a slightly higher PH than conventional water. Practitioners of traditional medicine have believed that alkaline water has potential benefits in disease prevention and longevity recently.

'Alkaline Water' was mentioned in the title of a peer reviewed, scientific journal (Journal of Medical Association JAMA Otolaryngol Head Neck Surg. 2017) for the first time since 1924. According to the paper alkaline water and Mediterranean diets are more effective than proton pump inhibitors (PPI's) the most commonly used antacids to treat Gastroesophageal reflux disease also known as GERD.

The article concludes that eating a Mediterranean diet and drinking alkaline water is a more effective treatment for GERD compared to over the counter acid reducers. The study participants did not take digestive support from herbs, enzymes or probiotics but still were able to achieve highly significant results with diet and alkaline water alone. Alkaline water is defined as having a pH around 8.0 and the Mediterranean diet is primarily plant based.

The importance of this is more significant as regular use of PPIs is in fact linked to several side effects including cognitive decline, cardiovascular disease and increased risk of infections. A paper published in J Environ Public Health in 2011 reported Alkaline pH of diet rich in plant food has a significance not only for digestion and longevity but also for heart health, cognition, cancer prevention, better outcomes during chemotherapy, bone and muscle building, availability of minerals, chronic back and joint pains.

Alkaline water can be produced by some special equipments or through natural spring or mineral water. Tap water is subjected to chemical treatments and chlorination which increases the damaging free radicals & oxidation which can cause damage to our cells and make us fatigued or diseased.

All in all alkaline water can play a huge role in elevating health and prevention of diseases. Alkaline water can be prepared in your kitchen with equipments available easily and also purchased ready made.

WAKE-UP TO COFFEE

If you thought, your favorite cup of coffee was unhealthy, think again!

Coffee's origin can be traced to the 12th century in Ethiopia, where it is believed to have been first harvested. 'Traders brought coffee to the Middle East, from where it began to spread outward in the 15th century, penetrating every corner of Europe over the next two hundred years'. Brazil is one of the largest coffee producing countries in the world.

The last few years, urban India has acquired a new coffee culture. International coffee chains are opening coffee shops and doing brisk business, even in smaller towns. While in South India filter coffee has been a tradition, India in general is waking up to coffee.

Coffee beans are cured either by air-drying or fermentation. The dried hulled beans are then roasted and ground. The green coffee beans have little flavour and aroma, until they are roasted. Beans expand to one-and-a-half times of their original size and become porous and are classified according to the colour of roasting into light, medium, dark, Italian or French roast which are very-dark.

Most coffee beans are harvested directly from coffee trees, while, a special variety called Kopi Luwaka also known as civet coffee beans are passed through the digestive tract of a cat-like animal called civet. The enzymes in the civet's digestive system break down some proteins that give the beans bitterness and its unique mellowness. Interestingly, this is the world's most expensive coffee, which typically sells for $200- $600/- lb. These treasured coffee beans come from Indonesia and other South-East Asian countries, and their supply is limited.

While there are several coffees, most of the world's coffee comes from two species-coffea Arabica and coffea Robusta. Both these kind of coffee bushes bear the fruit called cherry. Most cherries have two coffee beans in them, but a small percentage of cherries of the Arabica have only one coffee bean and this is the rare pea-berry bean. This pea-berry has much more flavor than its sister bean on the same Arabica plant, which is called the plantation bean. Arabica provides more taste and flavour, while Robusta, more body and caffeine. Chicory is added to give a rich dark colour to coffee. It is a green, the leaves of which are used in salad and the roots are dried, ground and roasted. It is sometimes added to coffee substitutes for a bitter taste.

Coffee that is available to us, may be a blend of as many as 5-6 different varieties of coffee beans. The blends are controlled for flavour, aroma, colour, strength or body. Blending is done by creative artists of the coffee world, who choose beans that combine to produce desirable brews. Once, a blend combination has been developed, it is continuously produced so that one coffee blend always has the same flavor or aroma. To prepare coffee, there are different methods, which include-filtration, percolation and steeping.

·Filtration, also called drip-method, water filters through the coffee powder into the lower compartment of the coffee maker.

·When coffee is percolated, heated water is forced upwards through a tube into the coffee compartment. The water filters through the coffee several times, before the coffee is of desirable strength.

·Steeping, the beverage is made by heating the coffee and water together but not allowing to boil.

Other forms of coffee include- decaffeinated, instant, iced and flavoured coffee. Many health conscious people have turned to de-caffeinated coffee, but there have been questions regarding safety of the decaffeinating process itself. Several de-caffeination processes are available including water, steam, carbon-dioxide, ethyl-acetate, methyl-chloride or coffee oils. However, now most decaffeinated coffee is made from methods which use water and steam with no chemical solvents and are therefore safe. Instant coffee powders contain dry, powdered water-soluble solids produced by drying very strong brewed coffee. The flavor of instant coffee is similar to that of freshly brewed coffee but the aroma is somewhat lacking in comparison with the freshly brewed beverage. These coffees should be kept packed in air-tight containers because they tend to absorb moisture.

Coffee contains more than 400 chemicals including trace amounts of vitamins, minerals and anti-oxidants. Caffeine is the main stimulant. A regular cup of coffee contains approximately 100 mg of caffeine. The caffeine content varies enormously depending on how strong the coffee is made. Caffeine increases epinephrine (adrenaline) release, which stimulates the central nervous system, increases states of alertness and increases heart-beat.

Despite, it's growing popularity, most people believe coffee to be somewhat toxic addiction taken only as an indulgence or to overcome sleep and boost alertness. Several, health concerns have been attributed to coffee drinking including it's addictive nature, ill-effects on digestion, bone health, cardiovascular health, disturbed sleep, high blood pressure, infertility and increased incidence in pancreatic or bladder cancer. Numerous studies now, however, reveal that coffee consumption and caffeine does not contribute to cardiovascular disease, including high blood pressure and stroke, even in people who drink more than four cups of coffee a day. Even though, coffee does cause a transient increase in blood pressure, moderate coffee drinking does not pose a significant risk to hypertensives. A recent study reports that coffee is a major source of dietary anti-oxidants and may inhibit inflammation and thereby lower the risk of cardiovascular diseases and other inflammatory diseases in post-menopausal women. Researchers have also found no link between coffee consumption and cancers of bladder, breast, colon, lung, pancreas and prostrate. Preliminary studies also suggest a protective role of coffee in liver cirrhosis.

Interestingly, numerous studies report that regular coffee consumption over long periods of time may reduce the risk of developing Parkinson's disease and Alzheimer's disease. In fact, a study on elderly revealed that coffee helped older people think better, improve their memory and reasoning skills. Caffeine may have a beneficial effect on weight loss as it has been shown to increase energy expenditure modestly. Caffeine being a natural stimulant may positively affect athletic performance. In one well-controlled study, subjects who ingested a high caffeine load one hour before exercise used less muscle glycogen and increased their endurance. However, there are no recommendations to use it as an ergogenic aid, as it is a diuretic and may aggravate loss of fluids. However, drinking large amounts may cause irritability and anxiety.

Inspite of the good news, drinking coffee carries some concerns. It is certainly habit-forming and even a single cup of coffee / day contains enough caffeine to create the risk of withdrawal. In some people, it can induce heart-burn by boosting up acid production. For pregnant women, coffee consumption has been linked to risk of miscarriages. Some studies have shown that women who consume 1-3 cups of coffee increase the risk of spontaneous abortion by 30%. Caffeine is a diuretic, which increases output of urine, which can be a concern for men with prostrate problems. Since it is a stimulant, it can contribute to difficulty in falling asleep and may interfere with regular sleeping pattern for many people and may cause disturbed or reduced sleep for some, therefore, those sensitive to it, should avoid coffee at bed time.

Cafestol and kahweol, compounds in boiled/ steeped coffee can boost cholesterol synthesis by the liver. These are found in highest concentrations in Scandinavian, Turkish coffees and French-press brews. Apparently, these compounds are trapped during filtration of coffee that is why people who drink filtered coffee don't have rise in blood cholesterol. Those with high cholesterol are advised to avoid boiled or

Drink	Serving size (ml)	Caffeine content (mg)
Coffee (drip method)	150	115
Coffee (percolator)	150	80
Instant coffee	150	65
Tea	150	40
Espresso	30	40
Decaffeinated coffee	150	03

steeped coffee and prefer drip or filtered coffee.

In a nutshell, it is better to use a moderate common-sense approach to coffee drinking. 1-2 cups a day should certainly not pose any risks for most people. Also, it does not increase the risk for any other health risk including heart disease, bone loss, cancer or infertility. People with irregular heart-beats (arrhythmias), pregnant women are advised non-caffeinated beverages. Since, coffee is a diuretic it must be avoided by individuals in sports as it can be dehydrating and affect their performance.

So, next time you go for your favorite cup of coffee, do it guilt-free, enjoy the ritual and stay alert. It can be enjoyed by all if taken in moderation.

GREEN TEA

Tea is the most highly consumed beverage in the world, other than water, as nearly two-thirds of the world's population drinks tea. However, unlike water, tea contains substantial amounts of polyphenols that have unique biological activities and may be responsible for many of the health benefits of tea. Currently there is wide interest in the medicinal benefits of green tea (Camellia sinensis).

Green tea is a 'non-fermented' tea, and contains catechins, vitamins polyphenols, water, carbohydrates, minerals .Catechins are strong antioxidants... However, during black tea production oxidation is promoted so that most of these substances are oxidized. Oolong tea is a partially oxidized product. Green tea is produced from freshly harvest leaves.

Recent human studies suggest that green tea may contribute to a reduction in the risk of cardiovascular disease and some forms of cancer, as well as to the promotion of oral health and other physiological functions such as anti-hypertensive effect, weight loss, antibacterial and anti virus activity, solar ultraviolet protection, bone mineral density increase, anti fibrotic properties, and neuro-protective power.

Green tea is a major beverage consumed in Asian countries primarily China, Japan, and a few countries in North Africa and the Middle East. The amino acid thiamine (5-N-ethylglutamine) is also unique to tea. Tea accumulates aluminum and manganese.

Nutritionist Ishi Khosla says Green Tea helps to
·Loose weight

·Decrease cholesterol absorption and plasma levels,

·Inhibits LDL oxidation,

·Reduce the adhesion molecule expression,

·Has antitrombotic activities by inhibiting platelet aggregation

·Decreases blood pressures.

Green tea is effective to prevent dental caries and reduce cholesterols and lipids absorption in the gastrointestinal tract, thus benefits subjects with cardiovascular disorders. As tea catechism is well absorbed in the gastrointestinal tract green tea is the most simple and beneficial way to prevent gastrointestinal disorders.

The polyphenolic compounds present in green tea show inhibitory effects on the induction of some cancers, notably, esophageal cancer. The protective compounds present in green tea may protect against cancer by causing cell cycle

Green tea is rich in polyphenolic compounds, with catechism as its major component. Studies have shown that catechism possess diverse pharmacological properties that include anti-oxidative, anti-inflammatory, anti-carcinogenic, anti-arteriosclerosis and anti-bacterial effects but polyphenols in tea may also increase insulin activity.

Tea, as normally consumed, was shown to increase insulin activity >15-fold in vitro in an epididymal fat cell assay. Black, green, and oolong teas were all shown to increase insulin activity. Addition of lemon to the tea did not affect the insulin-potentiating activity. Addition of 5 g of 2% milk per cup decreased the insulin-potentiating activity one-third, and addition of 50 g of milk per cup decreased the insulin-potentiating activity approximately 90%. Nondairy creamers and soy milk also decreased the insulin-enhancing activity.

Green tea is now an acknowledged cancer preventive in Japan. Epigallocatechin gallate (EGCG), the main constituent of green tea and tea polyphenols. EGCG and other tea polyphenols have been found to inhibit growth of human lung cancer cell line.

Thiamine in green tea may play a role in reducing stress. Furthermore, due to presumed antioxidant and anti-aging properties, tea is now finding its way into topical preparations. A growing body of research has demonstrated green tea polyphenols to be powerful antioxidants with anticarcinogenic properties. These polyphenolic compounds, specifically the catechins epigallocatechin-3-gallate (EGCG), epigallocatechin (EGC), and epicatechin-3-gallate (ECG), which account for 30-40 percent of the extractable solids of green tea leaves, are believed to mediate many of the cancer chemo preventive effects. Mechanisms of action may include antioxidant and free-radical scavenging activity, and stimulation of detoxification systems through selective induction or modification of phase I and phase II metabolic enzymes. In addition, green tea may inhibit biochemical markers of tumor initiation and promotion, including the rate of cell replication and thus inhibition of the growth and development of neoplasms. Current studies are hopeful, as they show an inverse association between green tea consumption and cancer risk, supporting a possible chemo preventive effect of green tea.

Based on the knowledge that green tea is inexpensive, non-toxic, and is a popular beverage consumed worldwide, clinical trials should be conducted to evaluate the in-vivo effectiveness of green tea polyphenols on the inhibition and chemo preventive treatment of cancer.

TEA

A legend tells us that one day in 2737 BC, a Chinese Emperor Shen Nung was boiling drinking water over an open fire and leaves from a nearby tea plant fell into the pot. The emperor drank the water and declared, it gave him vigor, contentment of mind and determination of purpose. Today that liquid beverage drunk throughout the world is second only to water. Tea is believed to have introduced into India around 500 A.D. by Prince Siddhartha, the one to become Buddha; he found it kept him alert during meditation and he brought the seeds to be planted in India. India subsequently became the largest tea growing country in the world. The Indians also developed their own "local" tea, "masala chai"- a fragrant warming tea.

The custom of tea drinking spread to Japan around 800 A.D. It was the Japanese Monks who created the wonderful ritual around drinking tea. In the year 1610 in Europe, tea was initially introduced as a medicinal brew. By 1700s, the Duke's wife began the tradition of afternoon tea to ward off hunger pangs between lunch and dinner. Asians used it for years together as a warm welcoming beverage for guests. Before long, its use spread and it became the most popular of all beverages, both for pleasure and medicinal purposes.

Tea in general, contains significant amounts of folic acid. Folic acid helps reduce the risk of heart disease and cancer. A person could obtain up to 25 percent of RDA for folic acid by drinking 5 cups of tea per day. However, tea drinking with a meal appears to have a negative effect on iron absorption due to presence of tannins. Tea is also rich in fluorine, useful for preventing tooth decay. A cup of tea provides about 0.3 mg. of fluoride. Tea contains small amounts of selenium, zinc and beta carotene, which are also antioxidants. The stimulant properties of tea can be attributed to caffeine, theobromine and xanthine, which also impart flavour. A single cup of tea provides half the amount the caffeine found in a cup of coffee. Tea can be grouped into three main types, black, oolong, and green tea. Coming from the same plant, the difference between both green and black tea lies in the extent of fermentation and oxidation. Green tea is non fermented tea and undergoes minimal oxidation compared to black tea, which is more oxidized, and generally stronger in flavor. Oolong tea is intermediate in composition between green and black teas.

Several studies have suggested that drinking either green or black tea may lower blood cholesterol concentration, blood pressure and inhibit clotting of blood, thereby providing some protection against cardiovascular disease. While green tea benefits arise from catechins, black tea benefits arise from theaflavins- both of which inhibit oxidation of bad cholesterol LDL .

Studies have shown that catechins in green tea renders various health benefits such as anti-oxidative, anti-inflammatory, anti-carcinogenic, anti-arteriosclerotic and anti-bacterial effects.

Since ancient times, green tea has been considered by the traditional Chinese medicine as a healthful beverage. Green tea is also known to prevent dental caries, reduce cholesterol and protect against certain cancers, especially esophageal and lung cancer. The polyphenolic compounds, specifically the catechins epigallocatechin-3-gallate (EGCG), epigallocatechin (EGC), and epicatechin-3- gallate (ECG) in green tea, are believed to mediate many of the cancer protective effects. Theanine, another polyphenol in green tea may play a role in reducing stress. Due to its presumed antioxidant and anti-aging properties, green tea is now finding its way into topical preparations.

A new addition to the range of teas is herbal tea. Herbal teas available in market, contain dried leaves of various plants other than tea. Often they are a mixture of several dried plant materials such as strawberry leaves, apples, hibiscus flowers, peppermint, ginger, nutmeg, cinnamon, chamomile and alfa-alfa; and various flavours may also be added. Herbal teas contain no caffeine but often contain substances that have soothing, stimulating or euphoric effects. Some potential health hazards are associated with their misuse. As has been seen, long term use of ginseng may produce hypertension, nervousness, sleeplessness and edema. So called dieters' or slimming teas may contain aloe, buckthorn and other plant derived laxatives that when consumed in excessive amounts, can cause diarrhea, vomiting, nausea, stomach cramps, chronic constipation, fainting and perhaps death. So stay away from any tea promising weight loss.

Milk in tea is largely a question of taste; however, some essential nutrients and some of the antioxidants may get bound. Avoid drinking at scalding (very hot) temperatures as it is risk factor for developing cancer of oral cavity. People suffering from ulcers or other inflammatory stomach conditions should avoid strong tea as it can lead to aggravation of symptoms.

Green/ black, both teas provide health benefits taken in moderation as a part of a healthy diet and lifestyle. Recently, increasing interest in the health benefits of green tea has led to its inclusion in the group of beverages with functional properties. Although evidence on green tea is promising, future studies are needed to better understand benefits of its regular consumption and contribution to human health.

MATCHA TEA

Teas are certainly not foreign to Indians, but the novel varieties being offered today, from green, white, and now matcha, are adding to the list of super-foods.

The brand new entrant is matcha tea – a concentrated form of green tea. Green tea is traditionally known to induce mental and cognitive function, physical activation and relaxation. Matcha, which is the ground-up form of green tea (and looks like Henna powder), is used in the Japanese tea ceremony. Drinking of 'matcha' tea, is actually the consumption of whole tea leaf as it is ground up into a fine powder giving the person drinking it 100% of the nutrients of the leaf. Although it has its roots in China, and later spread to Japan through Zen Buddhists, it is now found almost everywhere, and is frequently referred to as 'a mood and brain' food. Discovered by Buddhist monks wanting to stay alert during extended periods of meditation, Matcha is known to improve brain power without any of the downsides associated with other caffeinated drinks, and is being touted as a healthy alternative to coffee.

The two active principles of Matcha Tea include 'L-Theanine' and 'EGCG (a catechin)'.

High-grade Matcha Tea, which is one of the most expensive types of green tea, has the greatest percentage of L-theanine (an amino acid known to relax the mind, and decrease anxiety). It has been found to boost working memory, enhancing brain cognitive function. Caffeine content of matcha tea is also higher than that of green tea (about 35 mg per cup). This may also contribute to its alertness-enhancing properties.

Matcha Tea is grown in the shade and once harvested it is steamed to prevent oxidation, and to maintain its green colour. Studies have shown that matcha has greater potential health benefits than other green teas, owing to the levels of antioxidants (naturally occurring chemical compounds that prevent aging and chronic diseases). High antioxidant content translates to better protection against the formation of free radicals, which can damage tissues and cells.

Recent findings indicate that the concentration of the catechin epigallocatechin gallate (EGCG) available from drinking matcha is 137 times greater than the amount of EGCG available from regular green tea. EGCG is the polyphenol known for its ability to burn calories, and studied for its role in reducing cancer cell growth. It also fights inflammation, stimulates cellular repair processes, and contributes to the maintenance of healthy arteries.

Catechins are also found in foods like dark chocolate, berries and red wine.

Thought to be approximately ten times more potent than regular brewed green tea, matcha can raise energy levels, boost metabolism and help regulate blood sugar levels without the 'high and low' effect that caffeine can often have.

As per a study reported in the American Journal of Clinical Nutrition, consuming matcha green tea can increase thermogenesis (the body's own rate of burning calories) from a normal 8%-10% of daily energy expenditure, to between 35% and 43% of daily energy expenditure. This can certainly be an advantage to weight watchers, and those suffering from Metabolic Syndrome (belly fat, high blood pressure, diabetes, and heart disease). Preliminary studies suggest that EGCG has shown to have anti-cancer activity, and inhibit tumour growth, and Matcha, therefore, may help lower risk of certain types of cancers.

Many people use matcha in baked goods or smoothies, and since the taste can be grassy and a bit on the bitter side, a hot drink made with matcha is usually mellowed with milk and sometimes sweetened.

You may use matcha to add depth and flavour to a variety of recipes. Add a teaspoon to your morning smoothie/ vegetable juice/ soups, yogurt or oats, or porridge, to create a marinade or sauce for fish, chicken or tofu, or add it to cool, creamy desserts because of its highly concentrated nature, experts recommend keeping consumption of the same to two cups or less, daily.

All in all, a teaspoon of Matcha, added to your day's list of super-foods, can certainly help health and well-being, both physical and mental.

COLD-BREW COFFEE

If you had to put down your cup of coffee because of acidity or heartburn, there is good news. The cold brew coffee introduced recently in the market, offers you that caffeine kick without hurting you.

Cold brew coffee is not be confused with iced coffee (which is hot brewed coffee served over ice). Cold brew coffee is prepared when ground coffee is steeped in water (cold or at room temperature) for 12 to 24 hours to produce a concentrated coffee essence. This essence is diluted to taste and served hot or chilled. Cold brew can also be stored in the refrigerator for up to 2 weeks or frozen for a longer period, without its taste getting changed. Brewing coffee is dependent on various factors such as water volume, water temperature, size of the coffee particles (medium / coarse), the porosity of the coffee particles, and brewing time. The final composition (flavour, aroma, bioactive compounds) of cold brew is dependent on its brewing time. It is also believed that cold brew is smoother in texture compared to regular coffee. Cold-brew can be traced historically to 1600s, when the Dutch traders were looking for a way of producing coffee that traveled easily, while some believe that cold brew began recently in Japan and the U.S. Cold brew takes an edge over regular coffee due to its lower caffeine content and less acidic quotient. It is believed that cold brew has a caffeine content of about 40 mgs/100 gms as compared to about 60 mgs /100 gms in regular coffee. Cold brew coffee is known to have a ph of 6.3 compared to a ph of 5.5 of hot brewed coffee. Also, it has been claimed that an alkaline diet scores more with its health benefits as compared to a diet high in acid producing foods, including coffee.

Coffee contains more than 400 chemicals including trace amounts of vitamins, minerals and anti-oxidants and caffeine, the main stimulant. Caffeine increases epinephrine (adrenaline) release, which stimulates the central nervous system, increases states of alertness and increases heart-beat. Most people believe coffee to be somewhat toxic addiction taken only as an indulgence or to overcome sleep and boost alertness.

Numerous studies now, reveal that moderate coffee consumption (1-2 cups a day) and caffeine has certain health benefits and does not contribute to cardiovascular disease, including high blood pressure and stroke. In fact, coffee is known to be a source of certain dietary antioxidants.

Since it is a stimulant, it can contribute to difficulty in falling asleep and may interfere with regular sleeping pattern for many people and may cause disturbed or reduced sleep for some, therefore, those sensitive to it, should avoid coffee at bed time or try switching to cold brews. In fact, many health conscious people are turning to cold brews to get that caffeine kick and keep heartburn/ acidity in check. Despite the increasing popularity of cold brew coffee, more research needs to be conducted to validate its health benefits and or risks, if any.

KOKUM JUICE

The demand for fat burning pills seems to be growing for obvious reasons. What seems to have been missed is the fact that the most sought after popular fat burner Garcinia Indica is available right in our own backyards.

Popularly known as Kokum in India, Garcinia Indica has been used for centuries in Asian countries for culinary purposes as a condiment and flavouring agent in place of tamarind or lemon. It's used for juices, pickles and to add sourness to curries.

The Kokum tree is an evergreen tree predominantly grown in the tropical humid rain-forests of Western Ghats in South India. The fruits are green when raw and red to dark purple when fully ripe.

Kokum is widely used as a beverage and also has been used as medicine in traditional Indian Ayurveda.

A myriad of health effects have been attributed to Garcinia which range from anti-obesity effects, anti-inflammatory, anti-cancer to digestive benefits. The anti-obesity effects of Garcinia Indica come specifically from its hydroxy-citric acid (HCA) and have been elucidated in several studies over the past few decades. However, there are controversial results regarding it's efficacy and safety as an anti-obesity dietary supplement. Despite this, the market is flooded with plethora of over-the-counter slimming aids containing Garcinia & HCA.

A typical reduction of food appetite is reported and increased availability of mood enhancing neurotransmitter Serotonin has been observed in animal and human studies, with Garcinia. Besides this effect, it helps to enhance fat oxidation, reduces the tendency to store fat and leptin resistance. In other words, it suppresses fatty acid synthesis, formation of fat cells, food intake and induces weight loss. While, several studies report strong evidence, others show negative anti-obesity effects.

Besides weight loss, it is also found to be useful in treating obesity-related complications such as inflammation, oxidative stress, insulin resistance.

Kokum has been associated with several other nutritional and health benefits owing to its phyto-chemicals like anthocyanins and several other phenolic components. A recent animal study published in 2014 in the Journal of Biomedicine & Aging Pathology, reported intake of Garcinia improved ulcers, owing to its underlying antioxidant activity.

Another useful component of Kokum is Garcinol, which has been found to be neuro-protective, contributing to brain health and preventing dementia and Alzheimer's.

Different parts of this plant including its fruit, rind and seed have different applications in food and medicine. The rind is typically used for food and pharma industry while the Kokum seeds are used for making Kokum butter, which is often used in cosmetics and medicines.

While it is clear that Kokum and various parts of the plant have a role to play in weight loss and obesity management, it must be emphasized that there is no miracle or magic about it. A carefully planned diet and exercise are key to obesity management. Fat burners be it herbs, vitamins, minerals can only be supportive and work as adjuncts. The wisdom would be to take any of these in a natural form as food. When taken as supplements, it must be only under supervision. A glass of kokum juice is a cooling digestive beverage and certainly needs no prescription.

VEGETABLE JUICES

Any food borne mishap raises questions on food safety. The death of a woman after consuming bottle gourd juice has raised similar concerns.

Ironically, the reactions appear to die down as rapidly as they begin, for reasons best known to concerned people. Food safety is a fundamental need of an individual in an organized society. It affects each and every person – young, old, rich and poor. Yet, it is truly baffling why this indifference prevails and those involved in food production at any level get away with malpractices. Lack of public awareness coupled with corruption favours this growth of such unscrupulous food manufacturers – whether it is to do with microbial or chemical toxicity due to pollution, pesticide contamination and residues, antibiotics abd hormones or adulteration.

Let's take the example of the lauki (bottle gourd) juice. It's a low calorie, low carbohydrate beverage with moderate potassium and fiber content. Its good satiety makes it useful for weight watchers, diabetics, hypertensives and heart patients. What could have caused death of the woman on consumption of lauki juice remains unknown but the possibilities seem to be acute kind of toxicity from a natural toxin in the vegetable itself or a chemical or microbial contaminant which came from an external source. Whatever are the reasons, this incident of food borne mishap raises several relevant questions.

While most vegetables are safe to eat raw or cooked, natural toxins and anti-nutritional factors are well documented. Vegetables including broccoli, kale and cruciferous vegetables like cabbage, cauliflower and brussels sprouts harbour goitrogens (chemicals that suppress the function of thyroid gland and interfere with iodine metabolism). Eating large amounts of these raw are believed by some to worsen a pre-existing thyroid condition. Legumes including kidney beans and soybean contain toxic substances. Fava beans can be toxic to people who lack enzyme needed to protect red blood cells from damage by vicine, a toxic substance in fava beans that causes a type of anemia. Those taking monoamine oxidase (MOA) inhibitors to treat depression should avoid fava beans, as the combination can raise blood pressure. Green and sprouted potatoes contain alkaloids, called chaconine and solanine, which are poisonous and may trigger migraine or drowsiness in sensitive people. Alfaalfa sprouts too can be toxic and flare up symptoms for those suffering from lupus.

Likewise, several varieties of mushrooms can be toxic. Agaritine in mushrooms are toxins, but the good news is that cooking inactivates and reduces all these toxic substances and decreases the effect considerably. According to research, most natural carcinogens have long-term toxicity on prolonged exposure.

While most vegetables do not promote allergies some people

may react to members of the night shade family including eggplant, bell peppers and tomatoes.

Also, eating raw vegetables poses a risk of serious illness through microbial infection, most commonly E.coli and salmonella.

Excessive intake of certain fruits and vegetables too can be a problem. Fruits like apricots, prunes, are rich in sorbitol (a form of sugar alcohol) but can induce osmotic diarrhea, particularly in individuals sensitive to fructose.

It is commonly believed that bitterness is nature's protection from natural toxins in vegetables and fruits to mammals. However, bitterness needs to be qualified. A certain amount of bitterness in vegetables like karela, fenugreek or cucumber family (cucumber, squash, eggplants, melon, pumpkin and gourds) is normal and we are all accustomed to it. Tetracyclic triterpenoidcucurbitacins, complex compounds found in cucumber family are responsible for the bitterness in these vegetables. These are highly toxic to mammals, however, at what levels needs to be established. Higher levels of these chemicals are triggered by environmental stress, like wide temperature swings, low pH, high temperature, too little water, low soil fertility and improperly stored or over-matured vegetables.

Yet, vegetables and fruits are reservoirs of nutrients with numerous health benefits. In addition to antioxidants, vitamins and minerals, they also provide special disease fighting protective plant pigments called phyto-chemicals (phyto means plant) which have antioxidant properties. Some of the special nutrients include vitamin C, vitamin A,

B-complex vitamins, folic acid, vitamin E, K, potassium and fiber. These protect us from chronic degenerative diseases like cancer, cardiovascular diseases, diabetes, cataract, ageing, to name a few. Therefore, to become wary of eating these is not warranted. What comes through as an important learning is to follow the golden rule of "balance". Therapeutic doses of any food must be taken under the guidance of a qualified physician or professional.

What you can do:

• Vegetables and fruits must be purchased from a retailer source or reputed vendor. Make sure not to buy over-ripe/bruised fruits and vegetables.

• Avoid buying vegetables grown under unhygienic conditions.

• If something does not look or taste right, discard it.

• Wash vegetables & fruits thoroughly in saline water/potassium permanganate before consuming. If need be, peel them before consuming.

• Store under appropriate conditions. Vegetables including beans, eggplant, pepper and tomatoes that originate in warm climate, keep best at 50F (10C). Potatoes convert their starch to sugar below 40F (4C), keep them cool and out of the light to prevent the formation of poisonous alkaloids. Most other vegetables keep best at 32F (0C).

• Do not leave cut fruits and vegetables for long durations.

• Do not combine juices of naturally bitter vegetables with others.

• Avoid drinking juices, eating salads and cut fruits and vegetables outside the house from unhygienic vendors to prevent infections.

• Choose organically grown wherever possible. These contain fewer chemical residues and also retain phenolic compounds – chemicals that act as a plant's natural defense and also happen to be good for our health.

• Growing your own produce in your garden or farm is the best way to ensure that the fruits and vegetables you cat are pesticide free.

SUGAR

SUGAR: A DIETARY VILLAIN?

Inspite of being condemned as white poison, consumption of sugar seems to be increasing steadily. According to estimates, in India, per capita sugar consumption has tripled in the last 3 decades from 6 kg (1975) to18 kg (2000) per annum. Sugar consumption/ capita has also increased drastically from 3.4 kg (1700s) - 68.2 kg (2003) in U.K. The U.S. averages at about 40 kg of sugar per person per year.

It seems to be finding its way into drinks, sweets, chocolates, desserts and all kinds of goodies. Sugar enters our food also through several hidden names such as fructose, corn syrup, high fructose corn syrup, honey, jaggery, sucrose, lactose, maltose, dextrose, malto-dextrin, cane sugar, maple syrup, malt. (See table below).

Sugar is essentially a refined or simple carbohydrate. It is a source of calories i.e. it provides energy. It is easily digested and provides quick release of energy. It provides few nutrients if any, (with the exception of jaggery, honey, which may contain some minerals and enzymes) – therefore, often referred to as 'empty calories'.

While sugar may not be essential in diet (as all carbohydrates are eventually converted to sugar), it is a useful source of calories for physically active people, adds palatability to foods, and fixes the sweet tooth for many. Sweetened foods have been reported to be used as comfort food by emotional eaters. A calming effect is produced perhaps owing to the increased production of serotonin (a neurotransmitter).

Increased sugar intake through regular consumption of sweets, cakes, cookies, desserts, chocolates, sweetened beverages, fruit juices, fizzy drinks coupled with decline in energy expenditure as in the case of most urban lifestyles, can have negative effects on health.

Diets rich in sugars and refined carbohydrates can promote insulin resistance. Insulin resistance is a condition where the cells in our body do not respond or become resistant to insulin, a hormone that signals cells to absorb blood sugar. This prevents uptake of glucose into cells and leads to increased insulin levels in the blood.

Insulin resistance has been linked with a variety of problems including high blood pressure, high levels of triglycerides, low HDL (good) cholesterol, and excess weight. These can lead to type 2 diabetes, heart disease and possibly some cancers. Data from the Insulin Resistance Atherosclerosis Study suggests that cutting back on sugars and refined carbohydrates and eating more whole grains can improve insulin resistance.

In another study of 80,000 nurses, Harvard researchers found that low-fat, high-sugar diets, can worsen blood cholesterol, and triglyceride levels, both of which are risk factors for heart disease.

Interestingly, low-fat products on supermarket shelves are packed with sugar and refined carbohydrates to make up for the taste that is lost when fat is removed. Low fat cookies or breakfast cereals can be loaded with sugar. Also, many believe that low-fat alternatives are healthier and end up eating large quantities, which can worsen insulin resistance.

Often, we seek a sugary snack as a pick-me up when low on energy or tired. The truth is, that while there is an instant boost, excess sugar particularly among sedentary individuals in offices or on couches can lead to fatigue and exhaustion. Sugary snacks can also cause cravings for more, leading to weight gain. In fact, sweet cravings often indicate that you may be consuming excessive quantities of carbohydrates.

Another effect of excessive sugar intake is change in microbial flora in the gut. In the long run, this can eventually lead to bloating, and may worsen gastrointestinal complaints like heartburn, flatulence etc. Abnormal gut flora has also been linked to lowered immunity, allergies, skin problems like acne, eczema etc and compromised nutritional status. Sugar intake can deplete nutrients like B-vitamins, zinc and chromium.

Worldwide studies have shown that sugar is carcinogenic and undoubtedly the most important dietary factor in the development of dental caries. Foods that stick to the teeth, such as caramel, licorice, sugary cereals, sweetened beverages and cookies are more likely to cause dental caries.

According to current recommendations, added sugars ideally should be about 10% of the total caloric intake i.e. about 10 teaspoons in a 2000 cal. diet. While most of us enjoy the taste of sweet foods, habitually high sugar intake must be avoided. To moderate sugar in your diet:

• Fresh fruits, dry fruits like raisins, apricots, figs are preferred sweets.

• Use less white sugar, brown sugar, honey and syrups.

• Limit intake of soft drinks, sugared breakfast cereals, candies, ice creams, fruit juices, sweets and desserts.

• Use approved sugar substitutes, wherever possible.

• Read ingredients carefully. There may be hidden sources of sugar even in sugar-free foods.

• Treat celebration sweets with discretion.

FORMS OF SUGAR USED IN FOODS

• Brown rice syrup
• Brown sugar
• Concentrated fruit juice sweetener
• Confectioners sugar
• Corn syrup
• Dextrose
• Fructose
• Galactose
• Glucose
• Granulated sugar
• High fructose corn syrup
• Invert sugar
• Lactose
• Lactulose
• Maltose
• Mannitol

- Maple sugar
- Molases
- Natural sweeteners
- Raw sugar
- Sorbitol
- White sugar
- Xylitol

ARTIFICIAL SUGAR

Time and again I am questioned regarding safety of sugar substitutes. Newspaper reports, magazines and internet have only confused public on this issue. As a result, some consume it with apprehension and some give it up. I thought it was time to address this issue.

Sugar substitutes can be classified as nutritive or non-nutritive.

Nutritive sweeteners: Are those that impart sweetness to food and can be absorbed to yield energy in the body. These include white sugar, brown sugar, jaggery, honey, maple syrup, glucose, fructose, xylitol and mannitol. Fructose (fruit sugar) has the same calorie value as sugar but differs from sugar in the fact that it is absorbed more slowly than sugar.

Natural Sweeteners: Natural sweeteners such as honey contain fructose and glucose. Real maple syrup contains sugar (sucrose) from sugar maple trees. Most maple flavoured syrup commonly sold is made from corn syrup with added maple flavour added.

Refined Sweeteners: White table sugar is sucrose extracted from sugar beets or sugarcane.

Molasses is a by-product of the sugar refining process, but is itself unrefined. High fructose corn syrup tastes 1.5 times sweeter than table sugar and costs less to produce. It is therefore used in soft drinks and processed food.

Sugar alcohols: The sugar alcohols in sugarless chewing gums are also nutritive sweeteners but the body does not digest or absorb them fully, so they provide about half or less than half the calories compared to the other sugars. Sorbitol, xylitol , mannitol and maltitol are found naturally in food. These are additives in sugar free products such as gums, chocolates and mints. They are not as sweet as sugar and do not cause tooth decay. When sugar alcohols are used as the sweetener the product may be "sugar free" but it is not calorie-free.

Non-nutritive Sweeteners: Gram for grams, most of these are many times sweeter than nutritive sweeteners.

Saccharin Discovered in 1879 used in foods ever since, saccharin tastes about 300 times sweeter than sucrose. In the 1970s, research indicated that very large doses of saccharin were associated with bladder cancer in laboratory animals. As a result, in 1977 the U.S. Food Drug Administration (FDA) proposed banning saccharin from use in food. Widespread protests by consumer and industry groups, however, led Congress to impose a moratorium on the saccharin ban. Every few years, the moratorium was extended and products containing saccharin, had to display a warning label about saccharin and cancer risk in animals. In 2000, convincing evidence of safety led to saccharin's removal from the National

Toxicology Program's list of potential cancer-causing agents and the U.S. Congress repealed the warning label requirement. Aspartame Marketed as "Equal" The artificial sweetener aspartame is a combination of 2 amino acids, phenylalanine and aspartic acid. When digested and absorbed it provides 4 kilo-calories per gram, However aspartame is 200 times sweeter than sucrose (table sugar) that the amount used to sweeten foods contributes virtually 0 calories to the diet. It does not promote tooth decay. The FDA approved aspartame for use in some foods in 1981, for use in soft drink in 1983. More than 90 countries allow aspartame in products such as beverages, gelatin desserts, gums and fruit spreads. Because heating destroys the sweetening power of aspartame, this sweetener cannot be used in products that require cooking.

Several safety concerns have been raised regarding aspartame. Some groups claim that aspartame could cause high blood levels of phelylalanine. In reality, high protein foods such as meats contain much more phenylalanine than foods sweetened with aspartame. Even tomato juice contains phenylalanine. The amounts of phelylalanine in aspartame sweetened foods are not high enough to cause concern for most people. However, people with a genetic disease called phenylketonuria (PKU) cannot properly metabolize the amino acid phenylalanine so they must carefully monitor their phelylalanine intake from all sources including aspartame.

Although some people report headaches, dizziness seizures, nausea, or allergic reactions with aspartame use, scientific studies have failed to confirm these effects and most experts believe aspartame is safe for healthy people. The

FDA sets a maximum allowable daily intake of aspartame of 50 milligrams per kilogram of body weight. This amount of aspartame equals the amount in sixteen 12-ounce diet soft drinks for adults 8 diet soft drinks for children.

Aspartame in fact has been one of the most rigorously researched sweetener due to its extensive use in the past 20 years. Several scientific bodies including the European Food Safety Authority, WHO and USFDA have conducted extensive research. There has been no substantial evidence to show that aspartame is unsafe for children or adults. It is only in India that it is not recommended for children , simply because the guidelines suggest that children need extra calories for growth and therefore sugar substitute are not desirable for growth. This is not warranted. In fact it may be a useful tool to reduce weight and add variety to diabetic and obese children's diets.

Acesulfame K: Marketed under the brand name Sunette, Acesulfame K is about 200 times sweeter than table sugar. The FDA approved its use in the U.S. in 1988. Acesulfame K provides no energy, because the body cannot digest it. Food manufactures use acesulfame K in chewing gum, powdered beverages, mixes, nondairy creamers, gelatins, and puddings. Heat does not affect Acesulfame K, so it can be used in cooking.

Sucralose: Sold under the trade name Splenda, Suralose was approved for use in the U.S. in 1998 has been used in Canada since 1992.

Sucralose is made from sucrose ,but the resulting compound is non-nutritive and about 600 times sweeter than sugar. The process involves chlorination in the presence of phosgene gas. Sucrolose is often referred to as low calorie chlorine. Sucralose has been approved for use in a wide variety of products, including baked goods, beverages, gelatin desserts and frozen dairy desserts. It also can be used as a "table-top sweetner", with consumers adding it directly to food. The prescribed limit is 2.4 mg per kg body weight per day.

Other Sweeteners: D-tagatose An artificial sweetener derived from lactose that has the same sweetness as sucrose with only half the calories. It has 1.5 calorie/gram.

Trehalose: A sugar of two glucose molecules, but with a chemical linkage different from maltose. Used as a food additive and sweetner.

Neotame: An artificial sweetner similar to aspartame, but one that is sweeter and does not require a warning label for phenylketonurics.

STEVIA

Stevioside commonly known as stevia, relatively new to the list of sugar substitutes is used as a non-caloric sweetener in several countries. Native to South America, stevia is extracted from Stevia rebaudiana leaves. These plant leaves have been used as a sweetener since 1970's. Stevia is available as a dietary supplement in the United States, and has not been yet approved for use as a sweetener by US FDA (Food and Drug Administration, United States).

The leaf of the stevia plant contains certain compounds, most abundant being stevioside and rebaudioside A, that give it sweetness. These compounds are about 250-300 times sweeter than sugar but their metabolism in the body has not been completely investigated. A number of studies have suggested that, besides sweetness, stevioside along with other compounds may also have anti-hyperglycemic (blood sugar lowering), anti-hypertensive (blood pressure lowering), anti-inflammatory, anti-tumor and immuno-modulatory actions. However, more research is needed to validate these benefits.

Stevia is considered a good substitute to regular table sugar because stevia is sweeter and has zero calories. According to EFSA (European Food Safety Authority) panel on Food additives and nutrient sources, the Acceptable Daily Intake of stevia was determined at 4mg/kg body weight (measured as steviol equivalents), a level consistent with that already established by the Joint FAO/WHO Expert Committee on Food Additives (JECFA). This intake is set with a wide margin of safety and no adverse effects have been seen in intakes of stevia 100 times greater than the acceptable daily intake.

FDA has not actually declared stevia as a sugar substitute but rather only certain highly refined stevia preparations that contain rebaudioside A as 'generally recognized as safe' (GRAS), which means that they can be used as sugar substitutes. In general, products marketed as 'Stevia' are whole leaf Stevia or Stevia extracts of which rebaudioside A is a component. These highly refined stevia extracts may cause mild side effects, such as nausea or a feeling of fullness in some individuals.

FDA has not permitted the use of whole-leaf stevia or crude stevia extracts as food additives because of concerns about potential health effects. Among these concerns are the effects of stevia on blood sugar control, kidneys, cardiovascular and reproductive systems.

Remember that the daily allowance of sugar substitutes such as refined stevia preparations may be way above our intake, yet, a prudent approach is desirable.

ALCOHOL

Alcohol consumption has been a subject of much controversy. Historically, it has been a part of all ancient cultures. It's

Caloric Content of Typical Alcoholic Beverages						
		Carbohydrates		Alcohol		Total
Beverage	Amount (ounces)	Grams	Calories	Grams	Calories	Calories
Beer, regular	12	13	52	13	91	150
Beer, light	12	7	28	11	77	109
Beer, non alcoholic	12	12	48	1	7	55
Beer, alcohol free	12	12	48	0	0	48
Wine, table	4	4	16	12	84	100
Liquor (vodka, gin, rum, whisky)	1.25	0	0	14	98	100

* The small discrepancies in the calculation of total calories for beer and liquor may be attributed to a small protein content in beer and trace amounts of carbohydrates in liquor.

effect on health and larger social issues has been a subject of much debate.

Over the last two decades, based on epidemiological and clinical studies, scientists and healthcare professionals have agreed this low nutrient beverage in moderation (one to two small drinks a few times a week) offers benefits to reduce the risk of heart attacks and strokes. Although, its protective effects against coronary heart disease and diabetes were known, alcohol consumption in general has not been favoured in the general population as a recommendation.

The association appears complex. Researchers have recognised alcohol use as a leading risk factor for diseases linking its consumption to 60 acute and chronic diseases. A recent large new global study published in the Lancet in 2018 shows that there is no safe level of alcohol consumption. This study covered 195 countries and locations, and was followed up from 1990-2016 for both men and women. The study reported that alcohol use is a leading risk factor for diseases worldwide, accounting for nearly 10 percent of global deaths and the safest level of drinking is none. It was also reported that beyond 50 years of age, cancer accounted for a large proportion of total alcohol attributable deaths.

So, how is it that this much loved beverage has lost its beneficial effects? The issue could be a loss of tolerance by our bodies more than the beverage itself. With modern diets, food allergies and lifestyles, our digestive tract (gut) has undergone changes. Increased permeability, inflammation and changed gut microbiome are most likely the reasons for the loss of tolerance of alcohol by the human body and may explain the increased disease risk by alcohol consumption. Alcohol in itself injures the gut lining causing gut inflammation.

This interferes with nutrient uptake and may increase absorption of toxins in the blood. All in all, given the pleasure linked with moderate drinking, not drinking at all is unlikely to be complied with. The combination of good gut health and diet which is anti-inflammatory will help improve tolerance and perhaps reduce overall risk. Yet the message is clear, there is no safe level for alcohol consumption and if you must, keep it to the lowest levels. Those with inflammatory disorders like cancer, obesity, diabetes, digestive issues etc. must adopt a prudent approach.

HANGOVER
THE MORNING AFTER

After a night of drinking and carousing you wake up with a pounding headache, exhausted and sick. You obviously have been struck by a hangover. You may feel depressed, anxious, irritable or sensitive to light or experience muscle and joint pains. Perhaps it's nature's cry to tell you that 'you went wrong'.

Hangovers are no fun and may even last a couple of days. Just a few tips on prevention and to get you up and about.

Usually, a hangover begins within several hours after the last drink, when blood alcohol level is dropping. Symptoms normally peak about the time alcohol level reaches zero, and may continue for an entire day.

Alcohol may cause:

• Dehydration, leading to headache, dry mouth and electrolyte imbalance.

• Irritation of the stomach and intestines, contributing to stomach pain, nausea and vomiting.

• Hypoglycemia (fall in blood sugar levels) leading to lethargy and lack of energy, which could be serious for diabetics.

• Disturbed sleep patterns and biological rhythms contributing to fatigue.

• Irregular heart-beats (arrhthymias).

Blood levels of C-reactive protein, a marker of inflammation, are elevated and strongly associated with hangover severity.

Factors, other than 'only alcohol', that can worsen hangover are:

• Congeners (toxic chemicals formed during fermentation) in most alcoholic beverages are widely responsible for headaches and vicious hangovers. For example, congener methanol.

• Use of drugs, especially nicotine through cigarette smoking.

• Personality traits such as neuroticism.

• Negative life events and feelings of guilt.

Research shows that gin and vodka, beverages that contain less of the biologically active compounds cause fewer headaches. Contrary to popular opinion, combination of different alcoholic beverages is unlikely to cause hangover except if you have consumed too much.

So what can you do about your hangover?

• Drink plenty of water before going to bed to safeguard from ill effects of hangover. Fresh lime water, juices, coconut water, plain sodas can be beneficial.

• Taking vitamin B6 or an extract from Optunia ficus indica (a prickly pear cactus) before drinking may reduce the severity of hangover. A simple B vitamin supplement would do.

• Eating bland foods that contain complex carbohydrates, such as toast and crackers, can combat low blood sugar and possibly nausea. Do not take alcoholic drinks on an empty stomach.

• Adequate rest and sleep can ease fatigue.

• Drinking non-alcoholic, non-caffeinated beverages can alleviate depression. Contrary to popular belief caffeine can worsen symptom as it is a diuretic and increases urine production.

• Time is the most effective treatment; symptoms usually disappear in 8–24 hours.

• Certain medications can also relieve some symptoms. Antacids, for example, may relieve nausea and stomach pains. Mild pain killers may reduce headache and muscle aches, though, they may cause stomach irritation.

Use of medicines like pain killers and non-steroidal anti-inflammatory drugs can be dangerous particularly for heavy drinkers as it can increase the risk of liver damage and stomach bleeds. Therefore, alcohol should be taken in limited amounts. Frequent hangovers that are cured by another drink often called 'hair of the dog' should be avoided because additional drinking may only enhance the toxicity of the alcohol previously consumed and extends the recovery time.

Hangover Symptoms:

• Fatigue, weakness, and thirst
• Headache and muscle aches
• Nausea, vomiting and stomach pains
• Decreased sleep, decreased dreaming when asleep.
• Vertigo and sensitivity to light and sound
• Decreased attention and concentration
• Depression, anxiety and irritability

- Tremor, sweating, increased pulse, and blood pressure.

Key recommendations:

- Those who choose to drink alcoholic beverages should do so sensibly and in moderation – defined as the consumption of up to one drink per day for women and up to two drinks per day for men.

- Alcoholic beverages should not be consumed by some individuals, including those who cannot restrict their alcohol intake, women of childbearing age who may become pregnant and lactating women, children and adolescents, individuals taking medications that can interact with alcohol, and those with specific medical conditions.

- Alcoholic beverages should be avoided by individuals engaging in activities that require attention, skill or coordination, such as driving or operating machinery.

METABOLIC SYNDROME

Abdominal obesity in combination with one or few of the following parameters- elevated blood pressure, low HDL (good cholesterol), high LDL (bad cholesterol), high triglycerides, impaired fasting or elevated blood sugar and a family history of diabetes, is referred to as metabolic syndrome, also called "Syndrome X". The early stages of metabolic syndrome include weight gain, waist size increase and hypertension. Most of the susceptible people have atleast 2-3 components of the metabolic syndrome and with advancing age they develop into full blown disease, if not addressed.

Simply put, metabolic syndrome is not a disease, rather is a combination of risk factors leading to obesity, diabetes and cardiovascular disease. Over the last 3 decades, substantial research has been done to explain the root causes and inter-relationships of obesity, diabetes and cardiovascular disease. Dr. Gerald Reaven in 1988 provided the basis for the concept of metabolic syndrome and insulin resistance as its underlying cause.

Being insulin resistant means, the body does not respond to the affects of the given quantity of insulin (the blood glucose regulating hormone), the way a normal body should. This means that your pancreas (insulin secreting glands) need to produce more insulin than normal to control your blood sugars when you eat carbohydrates (sugar or starch) or excessive calories. It results from an excess of insulin in blood (hyperinsulinemia), and resistance to its actions. Hyperinsulinemia and insulin resistance causes a cluster of risk factors including central obesity, abnormal cholesterol levels (high triglycerides, high LDL and low HDL), glucose intolerance, high blood pressure, high uric acid, which predispose individuals to cardiovascular disease. High uric acid in the blood can lead to gout and certain types of urinary stones, but is not felt as a risk factor for cardiovascular disease. People with insulin resistance also have a tendency for preferential deposition of fat in abdomen-the "abdominal, or central obesity". All obese people, to some degree are insulin resistant, however, people with abdominal obesity are far more insulin resistant. It has been shown that polycystic ovarian syndrome (PCOS) in women is also an insulin resistant state which results in irregular menstrual periods and infertility.

Besides central obesity, other visible manifestations of metabolic syndrome include darkening & thickening of skin in certain areas (behind the neck, under arms, thigh folds), skin tags, buffalo hump, abnormal breast development in boys, excessive hair growth in girls and women, to name a few. A combination of environment and genetic factors act together to cause metabolic syndrome. Obesity, insulin resistance, diabetes and cardiovascular disease are all about interaction of genes with environment. Although genes are very important in determining metabolic syndrome, however, over the past half century, increased sedentary lifestyle and unlimited access to calories have blossomed the genes of insulin resistance into an epidemic of metabolic syndrome.

Screening for metabolic syndrome is important because of its relationship with cardiovascular disease, hypertension and diabetes as it increases the risk to suffer a heart attack.

On the more positive side, there is evidence that it can be completely reversed with healthy eating, physical activity and stress management. It could be done by aiming to:

• Achieve or maintain ideal body weight: Balance "in-take" with physical activity or by eating light in the subsequent meals. Consume plenty of whole grains, pulses, nuts, seeds, fruits and vegetables. Limit intake of sweetened beverages and alcohol.

• Eat a healthy & nutrient rich diet providing good calories, include complex carbohydrates, good fat, high quality proteins and fiber. Consume plenty of whole grains, pulses, nuts, seeds, fruits and vegetables. Limit intake of sweetened beverages and alcohol.

• Restrict intake of high calorie, low nutrient, oily, sugary and salty foods (packaged and convenient snacks like biscuits, fried namkeens, burgers, pizzas etc.).

• Shop and snack smart: Choose roasted/ baked snacks, low fat dairy products, fresh fruits and vegetables etc.

• Encourage physical activity: Engage in minimum of 30 minutes to 1 hour of moderate intensity physical activity on most days of the week. Regular physical exercise, besides helping in maintaining good weight, has been shown to improve hypertension, blood lipid levels and insulin resistance.

• Manage your stress: The best time to learn how to manage your stress is before stress strikes you. Being optimistic, regular mediation, deep breathing exercises and yoga are some simple ways to manage our stress.

• Lifestyle changes including a low fat diet with restriction of free sugars & refined carbohydrates and regular aerobic exercise can save you many health problems in future.

METABOLISM AND WEIGHT LOSS

Unable to lose weight, the blame is usually on a slow metabolism. Is it possible to be overweight because of a slow metabolism. Probably not. While, there is such a thing as slow metabolism, it is rare. It is usually not behind what is being overweight or obese in most cases. Unbalanced diets and lack of exercise are the chief reasons for excess flab.

The hard fact is that a slow metabolism is rare and usually found in medical problems such as cushing's syndrome or an under-active thyroid. Remember, metabolic syndrome or pre-diabetes associated with insulin resistance is a different entity and should not be confused with slow metabolism.

Metabolism is a process by which your body converts what you drink and eat into energy. During this process, calories in food and drinks are burnt to release energy for work and body functions. Even at rest, the body needs energy for it's vital functions like breathing and pumping of the heart etc. The number of calories our body burns to perform these functions is known as basal metabolic rate, commonly called metabolism. Several factors determine your metabolic rate.

• Body size and composition: Individuals with more muscle or larger body frame burn more calories, even at rest.

• Gender: At same age and weight, men burn more calories than women because they have more muscle and less fat compared to women. Fat tissue burns fewer calories than does muscle.

• Age: As we age, though energy needs for our body's basic functions remains almost the same, muscle tends to decrease which may slow down the calorie burning.

• Food processing (thermogenesis): The process of digesting and absorbing food also accounts for about 10 percent of the calories we consume each day. These requirements usually stay steady and don't change.

• Physical activity and exercise: Of all the factors listed so far, physical activity and exercise seem to be the most variable factor that determines the number of calories we burn. Depending on the intensity, duration and the kind of physical activity, the number of calories varies for each individual. The more active we are, the more calories we burn.

Imbalance in the calories eaten and burnt, usually results in weight gain. We can balance our excesses by keeping a check on our energy intake and increasing physical activity.

While we can't possibly control our metabolic rate or boost our metabolism, we can definitely work towards a healthy and active lifestyle to avoid piling up extra kilos by watching your calories and stepping up physical activity. These may be done by:

- Including whole grains, pulses, low fat dairy, lean poultry, fish, fruits, vegetables, nuts and seeds.

- Limiting sugary foods, oily food, refined flour, polished rice, refined oils, and hydrogenated fats. Keep a check on alcohol & empty calories.

- Regular physical activity: At least 30-45 minutes of physical activity on most days of the week. It's a good idea to include some movement at work if you have a sedentary job. Taking stairs or parking farther away from your workplace are some of the simple ways to burn more calories. Aerobic activity helps burn calories, and strengthening exercises help you maintain and build muscle mass, so a combination always works best but must be done under professional supervision.

As muscle tissue burns more calories than fat tissue, it's advisable to increase muscle mass by including some strength training exercises such as weight lifting. Strength training exercises also help counteract muscle loss associated with aging.

It may not be a good idea to succumb to products like fat burners or supplements to enhance metabolism, as they may be counterproductive. Do inform your physician before embarking on any quick fix.

MELATONIN

With increasing prevalence of sleep related issues melatonin has gained popularity. Melatonin is a hormone that controls the body's circadian rhythm – an internal system that regulates sleep and wakefulness. It also controls blood pressure regulation and seasonal reproduction. The production and release of melatonin is controlled by darkness and is suppressed by light. Melatonin levels in the blood are maximum just before bedtime. Many of those who have trouble sleeping have been found to have low levels of melatonin. This explains why melatonin supplements have gained popularity among people suffering with insomnia. Research on older adults suggests that taking melatonin half an hour before sleep time may decrease the amount of time required to fall asleep. In fact melatonin was first isolated in 1959 by Dr. Lerner, a dermatologist who used it on himself & was the first one to report its hypnotic properties. Many people use supplements of melatonin to fight jet lag these days. According to studies, melatonin taken on the day of travel and a few days later helps to recover from disturbed sleep patterns during travel. It appears to be more useful when crossing more than 4 time zones and moving towards the east. However if timing is wrong, it may worsen adjustment. Many small studies have found benefits of melatonin to manage sleep disorders among night shift workers. However studies are small, conflicting and evidence is inconclusive.

Interestingly, melatonin also helps the release of female reproductive hormones and determines the timing of menstrual cycle and menopause. It has been used to treat menstrual irregularities like poly cystic ovaries syndrome (PCOS) and menopausal complaints. Besides being a hormone controlling the body clock, melatonin also has powerful antioxidant benefits. It is also used for treating arthritis, migraine headaches, stress, anxiety, heart disease, alcoholism and cancer. Recent studies also suggest that melatonin interacts with the immune system and possesses positive immunological effects. It has been reported to be useful in fighting infectious diseases including viral, HIV and bacterial infections.

A study published in Journal of Clinical Oncology in 2002 highlighted melatonin's potential use in cancer treatment. It appears that it protects healthy cells from radiation-induced and chemotherapeutic drug induced toxicity. Its anti-cancer benefits have been demonstrated in several clinical studies.

Melatonin has also been used in epilepsy management, depression and schizophrenia.

According to research published in 2012 in the Journal of Child Neurology, melatonin was found to be safe and effective for treating patients with epilepsy. Another research published in Journal of Pineal Research in 2010 highlighted the role of melatonin in sleep disorders, depression, anxiety and even glaucoma. Recent studies have shown a powerful and unique role of melatonin on central nervous system injuries.

Considering its anti-inflammatory and anti-cancer benefits, adequate levels of melatonin in the body would surely be essential to prevent cancer, making good sleep hygiene an important element in prevention of cancer.

Melatonin is also produced in plants where it is used to fight damaging oxidative stress. The foods rich in melatonin are cherries, bananas, tomatoes, pomegranates, asparagus, olives, olive oil, grapes, wine, broccoli, cucumber, corn,rice, barley and oats. The good news is, it that it can be naturally boosted in the body by doing regular exercise, yoga and meditation.

The downside of using melatonin is possible drowsiness the following day. Regular use can make you dependent and amplify insomnia and disturb natural synthesis by the body by desensitizing the gland. This could lead to potential increased inflammation.

However, while short term safety has been established and it is relatively non-toxic in pharmacological doses, it is best taken as a substitute of sleeping medicine with your physician's knowledge. Supplements are available as tablets and capsules which are synthesized from amino acid tryptophan. In some countries melatonin is treated as a neuro hormone and cannot be sold over the counter.

So far studies on melatonin are conflicting. Larger studies are needed to identify bigger therapeutic and anti-inflammatory use of this hormone.

POLYCYSTIC OVARIAN SYNDROME (PCOS)

More than 90% of obese women and nearly 35% women in their reproductive years are believed to be suffering from polycystic ovarian syndrome (PCOS), one of the leading causes of infertility. Increasing numbers of women are seen to be suffering from PCOS, perhaps due to rapidly changing lifestyles, particularly, altered diet and exercise patterns. The primary cause of this disorder remains unclear and till now there has been no consensus on it.

Young women who get diagnosed with PCOS commonly seek medical attention because of irregular menstrual or missed periods, obesity, infertility, acne, excessive hair growth and thinning of hair on the scalp. Symptoms vary with different ethnic groups.

In the last decade, it has been shown that PCOS is an insulin resistant state. This means that there is too much insulin which is likely to cause testosterone overproduction by the ovaries. High levels of testosterone lead to absence of egg release (anovulation), amenorrhea (missed periods), infertility, irregular menstrual periods, delayed and heavy flow. Some miss their menstrual periods for several months or years at a time.

PCOS has also been linked to several metabolic abnormalities like high cholesterol levels, high blood pressure and abdominal obesity. It increases the risk to developing type II diabetes, heart disease, endometriosis and cancer.

Weight loss is essential for obese women with PCOS. It has been shown that even a 10-15% weight reduction resulted in spontaneous conception in about 75% of obese infertile women with PCOS. Insulin sensitizing agents work as useful adjuncts to achieve goals.

A healthy diet consisting of controlled carbohydrates, good fat and lean protein is helpful. Carbohydrates with low glycemic index are recommended. Low glycemic index foods are digested more slowly and induce less insulin secretion. These foods include wheat bran, barley, oats, whole seeds, lentils, kidney beans to name a few. Low GI help lose weight, increase HDL, improve insulin sensitivity and improve PCOS. Excessively sweet fruits and fruit juices must be avoided, as also starchy vegetables such as potatoes. Restrict portions of polished rice, pasta, noodles, breads, idli and dosas. Avoid simple carbohydrates like sweetened beverages and candies.

Strangely, women with PCOS tend to crave carbohydrates, perhaps to a greater extent than women without PCOS. This could contribute to binge eating and weight gain in the long term. However, small frequent meals with evenly distributed carbohydrate load can help to overcome cravings and result in long term weight loss.

Lean proteins from pulses, soybean, tofu, egg, chicken and fish and lean cuts of meat are desirable. Proteins can also be obtained through nuts and seeds. Contrary to popular belief mono unsaturated fats are helpful in improving insulin levels and correct abnormal cholesterol levels.

Good fats including omega 3 fats (fish, flax seeds, walnuts) and mono unsaturated fats (mustard oil, olive oil, canola oil, groundnuts, almonds) are useful. Natural sources of fats from nuts and seeds are best way of obtaining good fats.

Avoid hydrogenated or partially hydrogenated fats found in margarines, shortenings, fast foods, bakery products using them and commercially available fried foods. They are sources of harmful trans fats which can worsen insulin resistance.

Useful herbs include Fenugreek seeds (methi seeds), cinnamon

(dalchini), bitter gourd (karela) and blackberry seeds (jamun).
Alcohol must be restricted as excessive alcohol can worsen
insulin resistance. Women who consume alcohol must restrict
it to one small drink and avoid sweetened cocktails. Cigarette
smoking should be strictly discouraged in all women with
polycystic ovary syndrome as it will increase the risk of heart
disease and diabetes.

Women must make lifestyle changes to overcome PCOS
with or without drug treatment. A suitable diet and exercise
regimen are the cornerstones of therapy.

FOOD SENSITIVITY: NON CELIAC GLUTEN INTOLERANCE

A protein called gluten in wheat, oats, barley and rye (European
cereal) is known to cause a condition called celiac disease. It is a
condition in which gluten damages the intestines and reduces
the ability of intestines to absorb food. The individuals with
this condition can manifest typical or atypical symptoms or
may have hardly any symptoms, also called silent celiacs.

Typical symptoms of celiac disease include diarrhea,
gastrointestinal disturbances like abdominal distension,
bloating, burping, reflux, flatulence, pain, constipation; nausea,
vomiting; growth problems; stunting, weight loss; anemia,
lethargy, tiredness. Atypical symptoms include bone and joint
problems like osteoporosis, arthritis, cramps, aches and easy
fractures; skin problems, infertility, recurrent miscarriages,
giddiness and imbalance, epilepsy, mouth ulcers, numbness,
tingling sensation and behaviour problems like depression,

anxiety, irritability and poor school performance. Absence of typical symptoms makes the diagnosis difficult and often leads to ill health and life threatening maladies. Celiac disease can creep up silently on just about anyone — across age, gender, class and race — and turn fatal if undiagnosed! Celiac disease is diagnosed through a simple blood test and confirmed through the gold standard intestinal biopsy, which shows damage to the intestinal lining (villi).

However, another form of sensitivity to wheat called non-celiac gluten sensitivity (NCGS) has been identified. The relatively new entity is now being recognized by healthcare practitioners and it is important to understand the difference between these conditions even though they may all respond to a gluten-free diet. You may develop it at any age even if you have been consuming gluten all your life.

Non-celiac gluten sensitivity has been coined to describe those individuals who cannot tolerate gluten and experience symptoms similar to those with celiac disease but who lack the same antibodies and intestinal damage as seen in celiac disease. Research suggests that non-celiac gluten sensitivity is an innate immune response, as opposed to an autoimmune or allergic reaction.

Individuals with non-celiac gluten sensitivity may also have a high prevalence of extra-intestinal or non-gastro-intestinal symptoms such as headache, "foggy mind," joint pain and numbness in the legs, arms or fingers. Symptoms typically appear hours or days after gluten has been ingested.

Non-celiac gluten sensitivity has been clinically recognized as less severe than celiac disease. It is not accompanied by enteropathy (intestinal damage), elevations in tissue-transglutaminase (tTg), endomysial or anti-gliadin antibodies, and increased intestinal permeability that are characteristic of celiac disease. Increased intestinal permeability permits toxins, bacteria and undigested food proteins to seep through the gastrointestinal barrier and into the bloodstream, and research suggests that it is an early biological change that comes before the onset of several autoimmune diseases.

Simply said, individuals with non-celiac gluten sensitivity would not test positive for celiac disease based on blood testing, nor do they have the same type of intestinal damage found in individuals with celiac disease. Some individuals may experience minimal intestinal damage, and this goes away with a gluten-free diet.

The word of caution is to seek professional help, if in doubt. Self diagnosis and going off gluten can lead to a missed diagnosis of more serious celiac disease. Although gluten-free diets are gaining popularity and are warranted in celiac disease, non-celiac gluten intolerance and some other conditions, it must not become a fad.

WHEAT AND INCREASING INCIDENCE OF CELIAC DISEASE AND GLUTEN RELATED DISORDERS

The alarming increase in celiac disease and gluten related disorders in the last decade, has led to much speculation both in the scientific community and public regarding the reasons. It seems that the dramatic changes in the symptoms and presentation of celiac disease and gluten related disorders have taken place when new cereal hybrids were introduced into our diet. This means that the changes in the gluten containing cereals themselves has been the principal cause. Sophisticated hybridization techniques have been used to produce new strains of modern wheat, which could be high-yielding, high-gluten, disease resistant or pest resistant. These have made their way into our food supply in the absence of human safety studies. It is believed that these newer varieties are highly immunogenic compared to earlier varieties. Physically too, the modern day wheat looks like a dwarf grass compared to the tall grass it used to traditionally be. It bears little resemblance to the traditional varieties, even in terms of its chromosomal uniqueness.

The first one genome wild wheat, also called einkorn, the great ancestor of all wheat in the world has the simplest genetic code of all wheat, containing only 14 chromosomes. Shortly after the cultivation of the first einkorn plant, the emmer variety of wheat (the natural offspring of parents einkorn and an unrelated wild grass) made its appearance in the Middle East, including 28 chromosomes. Modern wheat, however, is a 42 chromosome plant.

The first cultivation of wheat occurred about 10,000 years ago, as part of the 'Neolithic Revolution', which saw a transition from hunting and gathering of food to settled agriculture. These earliest cultivated forms were diploid (einkorn) and tetraploid (emmer) wheats and their genetic relationships indicate that they originated from the south-eastern part of

Turkey. Cultivation spread to the Near East by about 9000 years ago when hexaploid bread wheat made its first appearance. Currently, about 95% of the wheat grown worldwide is hexaploid bread wheat, with most of the remaining 5% being tetraploid durum pasta wheat.

The difference is not only physical. Disease triggering gluten proteins are indeed expressed to higher levels in the modern variety. Other factors such as total gluten intake, use of fertilisers and pesticides and genetic susceptibility also may determine development of celiac disease and gluten sensitivity. While improved diagnosis certainly is a factor, but it cannot alone explain the current epidemic of celiac disease. Wheat is listed among the top eight food allergens and adverse reactions to wheat and wheat protein can be in the form of an allergy, celiac disease, skin rashes (dermatitis) or intolerance also known as non celiac gluten intolerance (NCGI). Symptoms for allergies could be respiratory, asthma, atopic dermatitis, urticaria, and anaphylaxis.

Celiac disease is the chronic inflammation of the gut which leads to mal-absorption of food and symptoms can be diverse, ranging from diarrhea, gastrointestinal disturbances like abdominal distension, flatulence, pain, constipation; nausea, vomiting to growth problems, stunting and anemia, but not everyone presents with these. In-fact, only 50% cases may present with typical symptoms. Other symptoms include weight loss, lethargy, tiredness, bone problems like osteoporosis and cramps; skin problems, infertility, mouth ulcers, numbness and behaviour problems like depression, anxiety, irritability and poor school performance. Absence of typical symptoms makes the diagnosis difficult and often leads to ill health and life threatening maladies.

Symptoms and presentation of celiac disease and non celiac gluten intolerance are similar and are associated with auto-immune diseases.

With the increasing recognition of toxicity and ill-health associated with modern wheat, farmers, agriculturists, food industry, government and consumers may need to adapt to the new requirements. The exponential growth of the gluten-free market in the last few years globally cannot be ignored as yet another food fad.

Despite being talked about, there is little actual awareness about gluten and gluten-free foods in India. Gluten is a protein found in wheat. It is composed of two elements gliadin and glutenin and is responsible for the elasticity of the dough. Gluten is also found in other grains such as barley, rye, semolina and some varieties of oats. Some dietary supplements also have gluten.

Today, gluten-free food is readily available for those suffering from celiac disease (a condition in which gluten severely damages the intestines) and those with non-celiac gluten sensitivity (NCGS) – have difficulty tolerating gluten). But many adopt a gluten-free diet just as a fad.

Readily available at super marts, health food stores and pharmacies, gluten-free foods is becoming popular because it is often endorsed by celebrities and also because of the common perception that it promotes weight loss.

While going off gluten may have some benefits, it is not a panacea for all ills, nor is it a magic weight loss mantra.

SPROUTS – THE NUTRIENT CAPSULES

No prescription for health seems complete without a mention of sprouts making these tiny plants popular with nutritional experts. Perhaps the most exciting is the multiplication of nutrients by the germination itself. Sprouts, in fact can be called little food factories, for in them are manufactured vitamins and enzymes which were not there to begin with. These food factories also are equipped with digestive powers as they develop enzymes which break proteins into simpler forms of amino acids, fats into fatty acids and carbohydrates into sugars and starches, which can be digested by the body even without cooking. Thus, sprouting benefits digestibility too and provide partially digested food. The partial digestion of nutrients allows the consumption of sprouts as raw foods and without the need for cooking and/or with minimum cooking. Enzyme rich sprouts are also alkaline to the body unlike the original grains, lentils and seeds which are acidic in nature. Intense cooking destroys most of the delicate B vitamins, antioxidants and enzymes in food. Sprouts can be eaten raw or lightly cooked by sautéing or steaming. Sprouted soybeans should always be cooked before use, but all other sprouts can be eaten raw. Now that is truly incredible!

Sprouts are a perfect way to start the day and make nutritious snacks too. Almost anyone can enjoy sprouts but being low in calories and high on nutrition they are specially good for weight watchers. However, they should be avoided by those recovering from acute illness or gastrointestinal infections. These days, supermarkets and health food stores sell a variety of sprouts, but it's easy to make them at home – all you need is a jar, a square muslin cloth and a rubber band or a sprouter. Make sure they are prepared hygienically as they can be a source of bacterial infection.

Sprouting

• Use whole pulses, as split ones will not germinate. Large pulses such as chickpeas take longer to sprout than small beans, but they are all easy to germinate and will be ready in about 3 days.

• Wash 3 tablespoon pulses or grains thoroughly in cold water, place them in a large jar or better in an earthenware pot.

• Fill the jar/ pot with lukewarm water and cover the top with a piece of muslin cloth, secured with a rubber band. Leave in a warm place overnight.

• Next day, pour off the water through the muslin cloth and refill the container. Shake gently, then turn the jar upside down and drain well. Leave the container in a warm place away from direct sunlight.

• Rinse the pulses or grains in fresh water three times a day until the sprouts have grown to the desired size. Regular rinsing and draining helps to prevent beans from getting rancid. Rinse alfalfa, soybean and chickpea sprouts four times a day.

• Remove from the jar, rinse well and discard any ungerminated beans.

• After 2–3 days, place the jar in sunlight to encourage the green pigment chlorophyll and increase the magnesium and

fiber content.
• Store sprouts in a covered container in the refrigerator for 2–3 days.
• Rinse well in cold water before use.

Grains, seeds, pulses and cereals are largely devoid of vitamin C. Sprouting increases vitamin C by nearly 60% and generates vitamin C up to an amount that one serve is enough to meet the recommended adult's daily needs of 40 mg. One cup moong sprouts for instance, provide an impressive 70 mg of vitamin C, (100 gms orange provides 40 mg vitamin C). The vitamin B content of the grains also increases phenomenally, almost by 20–30% particularly B1, folic acid and biotin. Vitamin B6 and folic acid are useful in prevention of heart disease. Sprouting also increases bioavailability of proteins, vitamin E, potassium, phosphorus and magnesium. The remarkable part goes beyond this. Grains and pulses are known to contain certain interfering factors for the absorption of minerals like iron and calcium, (deficiencies of which are very common). Well-known inhibitors include phytates, trypsin inhibitors and tannins, which bind themselves to iron and calcium and make them unavailable. Sprouting destroys most of these interfering substances and allows easy availability of these minerals for use by the body. Iron absorption is further enhanced by the presence of high levels of vitamin C produced during sprouting. Interestingly, the process of sprouting beans is also known to breakdown certain carbohydrates which cause flatulence (gas), in sensitive individuals, thereby relieving them of this common side-effect of eating beans and pulses. Almost, any whole bean, pulse, seeds or grains can be sprouted. The most common sprouts remain moong bean, black-gram (kala channa), moth, chickpeas (safed channa), alfalfa, sunflower seeds and fenugreek (methi). Soybean sesame seeds (til), millets are all good for sprouting. Sprouted beans, lentils and peas tend to have a denser, more fibrous texture than sprouts grown from seeds, which tend to be more delicate, are an excellent addition to soups, salads, stir fries and many Chinese and Asian dishes. Alfa alfa sprouts have special benefits as they contain compounds called saponins. Saponins have been found to lower bad cholesterol, thus useful in protection against cardiovascular disease. Sprouts are best eaten raw as they retain their crunchy texture and are not suitable for cooking.

Sprouts can be thrown into salads, sandwiches and fillings or stir fried with seasonal vegetables like carrots, red and yellow peppers, mushrooms, celery, onions etc. They can be used in savoury tangy chaats as well. Sprouted grains make an excellent addition to breads, giving them a pleasant crunchy texture. Grain sprouts can be kneaded into the dough after the first rising, before shaping the loaf or placing the loaf in the tin. Sprouts can be ground to make pancakes (chilla) or cutlets (tikki). Use a mixture of different types of sprouts for a variety of taste and texture.

GRAIN SELECTION/ CARBOHYDRATES/ LEAKY GUT

Our gut, or the intestine, is about a twenty feet long organ believed to be until recently, the seat of digestion. It regulates our uptake of nutrients and how we feel after eating food.

It's not surprising that traditional healers and practitioners of medicine, including Hippocrates (the Father of Modern Medicine), claimed that all diseases begin in the gut. The gut has a barrier function and also plays a role in protecting our bodies from toxins and undesirable elements. In the recent past, the gut has also been linked to our immune system, our nervous system and even our hormonal balance. This means that any impairment or inflammation in the gut will impact our nutrient absorption, our moods, and our immune health.

Under certain circumstances, the integrity of the gut gets compromised. This could be due to inflammation and change in balance of good and bad microbial flora (microbiome).

Normally, intestinal cells are glued together by so-called tight junctions. They prevent undigested food and toxic substances from crossing over to the bloodstream. If the gut barrier is impaired, the tight junctions may break up, increasing the permeability of the gut, leading to what is commonly called 'The Leaky Gut Syndrome'. This condition is held responsible for development of several food intolerances and allergies, and is associated with chronic fatigue, foggy brain, neurological disorders, migraines, epilepsy, ADHD (Attention Deficit Hyperactivity Disorder), lowered immunity and auto-immunity, skin and hair problems like dermatitis, urticaria, eczema, psoriasis, hyper-pigmentation, fibromyalgia (muscle pains, joint pains), Inflammatory Bowel Disease, constipation, acid reflux, and bloating. Even hormonal imbalances leading to polycystic ovaries (PCOS) and infertility, can be traced to a leaky gut. Serious health maladies like celiac disease, tumours and malignancies, are also associated with increased gut permeability.

The gut barrier faces continuous ongoing aggression because of ageing, infections, alcohol abuse, medicines, antibiotics, pesticides and heavy metal toxicities, high-sugar and high-carbohydrate diets, and chronic stress.

Bacterial toxins (endo-toxins) and ingested toxic material can also injure the intestine, making it more porous. Toxins may find their way into the body and burden the immune system, compromising the immunity and increasing inflammation. Circulating antibodies and toxic residues can trigger auto-immune reactions leading to auto-immune health conditions such as rheumatoid arthritis, thyroid disorders, multiple sclerosis, vitiligo, lupus, etc.

Treatment involves eliminating the underlying causes, improving diet, reducing alcohol, limiting sugars, processed foods, trans-fatty acids, and including antioxidant-rich foods, good fats (omega-3 fatty acids), prebiotics and probiotics, into the diet.

Regulation of gut permeability by diet has also been found to be positively impacted by vitamin-A, vitamin-D, calcium and magnesium status.

Special fats like butter and ghee, which contain butyrate, and medium-chain triglycerides (MCTs) in coconut have been found to repair the leaky gut. Addition of green-leafy vegetables and millets also improves the mucosal damage.

GUT AND BRAIN

THE GUT FEELING

If you thought, that you had one brain in the head which controlled how you feel and your decisions, think again! According to some recent research, there exists another little brain in our gut. This little brain appears to control a lot of how we feel, what we choose to eat and puts us in touch with our insides.

All of us go through the experience of giving into temptation and dig into unhealthy food knowing fully its conflict with our health goals. Obviously the information stored in our brain is not enough to control our eating behaviour. The second brain in our bowels, consisting of about 100 million neurons, controls several aspects of eating – these include mood regulating hormones, several neurotransmitters including serotonin, appetite regulating hormones including ghrelin, neuropeptide YY and digestion controlling neurotransmitters. This could have far reaching implications in management of body weight, mood, immunity and digestive disorders like IBS (irritable bowel syndrome).

In other words, the second little brain in the gut in connection to the big one in the skull determines our mental state and plays a key role in certain diseases throughout the body. The second brain however, is not the seat of any conscious thoughts or decision making.

While, it is well known that the brain in the head sends signals to the rest of the body, it seems that our second brain in the gut works the other way round and sends information from the gut to the brain. Equipped with its own reflexes and senses, the second brain can control digestion and gut behaviour independently of the brain. In other words, the brain in the head doesn't need to get its hands dirty with the messy business of digestion.

A big part of our emotions are probably influenced by the nerves or the brain in our gut. Our gut feelings and butterflies in the stomach literally seem to be rooted from there. The second brain informs our state of mind to the brain in the head in obscure ways. Scientists are learning that 95% serotonin secreted by the body is found in the bowels. Serotonin in the body plays a role in several diseases. Too much serotonin causes symptoms that can range from mild shivering or diarrhea to severe symptoms as muscle rigidity, fever or seizures. It is no wonder that conventional treatment involving altering serotonin levels provokes gastrointestinal issues as a side effect. Irritable bowel syndrome, one of the most common digestive disorders, arising in part from too much serotonin in our intestines could perhaps be regarded as the mental illness of the second brain. This information may be useful in regulating our emotional well being and treatment of stress and depression. Ultimately, this could lead to modifying your eating behaviour through our gut.

The second brain also seems to be working with the immune system protecting us from hostile bacteria. Its role in immunity and inflammation are exciting areas of research.

The second brain is complex and complicated, however, offers a whole new area of research for understanding our eating behaviour and potential treatment modalities in the future.

INTERMITTENT FASTING

The magic bullet for fighting flab is still waiting to be found and chances are it could be a while! The truth is, it is simply impossible to oversimplify or package solutions to complex eating patterns, diet and food facts in a formula.

Though most diet and exercise trends have their origins in science, the facts tend to get distorted by the time they achieve public popularity. Benefits are exaggerated. Risks are downsized. Science and prudence get overshadowed.

For almost a century proponents of 'breakfast being the most important meal gave birth to a whole industry around sugar laden breakfast cereals. Breakfast was promoted as foundation and pre-requisite to good health. Many people who did not feel comfortable eating in the morning started stuffing themselves up to adopt a healthy habit. Another popular weight loss mantra that has been around is small frequent meals and eating every two hours. With the growing popularity of intermittent fasting (IF) the wisdom of both these hugely popular concepts of good health have been demolished. Obviously these and the numerous other conflicting diet theories including calorie counting are simply not working to combat the obesity explosion. Time and again a new diet mantra appears and promises to be the fix. We hope that intermittent fasting does not meet the same fate. Intermittent fasting is a term that allows you to eat within a period of few hours and fasting for the balance. Typically it involves an eight hours period of eating. Common intermittent fasting method involve daily 16 hour fasts or fasting for 24 hours, twice per week fasting as a concept is not new and has been acknowledged as valuable practice by traditional health practitioners. As a matter of fact Gandhiji, the Father of the Nation, believed in fasting as a means to keep the body healthy. He practiced fasting not only to strengthen his body and soul but also as a means to fight for his goals.

Science has now established that fasting has definite health benefits for the body and the brain. If done properly it gives the body time to recover, rest and detoxify. It helps clearing metabolic waste, restoring digestive health and prevents constipation. One of the great benefits of fasting besides weight loss is autophagy. The 2016 Nobel Laureate Dr Yoshinori Onsuni (a cell biologist at the Tokyo Institute of Technology) has discovered the physiological process called autophagy through which the body degrades (breaks down) and recycles damaged cells, proteins and toxins. It has being linked to numerous health benefits including lowering inflammation, improved digestion, reduce risk of cancer, neurological disorders, balance lipid, blood sugar, blood pressure and stress.

According to researchers without autophagy our cells won't survive. Fasting has been shown to improve biomarkers of disease, reduce oxidative stress and preserve nerve cells, learning and memory functioning, According to Dr Mark Mattson, a neuroscientist from the National Institute on Aging and a professor at John Hopkins University USA intermittent fasting and calorie restriction in obesity, asthma, cancer and inflammation have found great benefits. According to a published study by Dr Mattson overweight adults who adhered to the intermittent fasting diet lost 8% of their initial body weight over eight weeks. They also saw a decrease in markers of oxidative stress and inflammation, and improvement of asthma-related symptoms and several quality-of-life indicators.

In another study, Mattson and colleagues explored the effects of intermittent and continuous energy restriction on weight loss and various biomarkers (for conditions including breast cancer, diabetes and cardiovascular disease) among young overweight women published in the international Journal of Obesity 2011. They found that intermittent restriction was as effective as continuous restriction for improving weight loss, insulin sensitivity and other health biomarkers. Intermittent fasting improves memory, learning functionality and slows ageing of the brain. It appears to be a relatively more sustainable approach and effective without the burden of calorie counting.

However, over enthusiastic followers may actually lose out on the legitimate benefits of fasting. A concern is that promoters of intermittent fasting can also encourage feasting or extreme behaviours such as bingeing. Often people are shown eating heaps of high-calorie, high-sugar high fat junk food in the eating phase implying if you fast two days a week, you can devour as much junk as you like during the remaining five days.

So what needs to be encouraged is a healthy diet and not unhealthy junk. Calorie restrictions and prudent choices must be an outcome of the diet. According to research the benefits will accrue only when there is overall reduction in calorie intake (if, that is, you don't over-eat on non-fasting days) which could create a caloric surplus instead of a deficit). The eight hours of eating should ideally be tuned with the circadian rhythm or body clock. Eating according to one's peak hunger time and in the early part of the day rather than later must be emphasized. Else it can lead to late night bingeing which can be counter-productive.

It also needs to be adapted for those with unstable blood sugars, diabetics on insulin, people with serious health conditions and sports persons. The diet should also consider food sensitivities and one size fit all approach is unlikely to succeed.

Tips to achieve weight loss and health goals with intermittent fasting

• Eat healthy, avoid sugars and refined grains. Instead, eat fruits, vegetables, beans, lentils, healthy grains, proteins, and healthy fats (Mediterranean type of diet).

• Allow the body to burn fat between meals. Don't snack. Be active throughout your day. Build muscle tone through yoga, light weights and some form of aerobic physical activity.

• Consider a simple form of intermittent fasting. Limit the hours of the day when you eat, and for best effect, make it earlier in the day (between 7 am to 3 pm, or even 10 am to 6 pm, but avoid the evening before bed).

• Limit snacking or eating all the time, especially at night.

RECIPE FOR LONGEVITY

We cannot be disease-proof or immortal but certainly, we can add life to our years and years to our life. What long-lived healthy people and cultures have in common, helps researchers to discover the secrets of youthfulness and longevity.

Some of the longest-lived cultures include Abkhasia (ancients

The traditional diets of the long lived cultures			
	Abkhasia	Vilcabambans	Hunza
Percent calories from			
Carbohydrates	65	74	73
Fats	20	15	17
Proteins	15	11	10
Overall daily calories (adult males)	1900	1800	1900
Percentage of diet			
Plant Foods	90	99	99
Animal Foods	10	1	1
Consumption			
Salt	0	0	0
Sugar	0	0	0
Processed Food	0	0	0
Incidence of Obesity	0	0	0
			(Robbins J, Healthy at 100)

of Caucasus, ancient USSR), Vilcabambans (Andes, South America), Hunza (Pakistan), Centenarians of Okinawa (Japan), Crete (Greece). Okinawa is home to the world's healthiest elders with longest recorded life expectancies. Scientific studies and research have some amazing conclusions and similarities. It appears that besides genetic factors, longevity is strongly linked with food and exercise habits. Low calorie healthy diets and high physical activity of these extraordinarily healthy societies are the secrets for their extended lifespans with virtually no reported incidence of diseases like high blood pressure, heart disease, cancer, diabetes and other degenerative diseases such as rheumatism, osteoporosis, Alzheimer's and vision problems. Not only this, these populations have been found to look youthful, exceptionally cheerful, happy and full of zeal even in later years. Most of them even work in the fields even at 120 years or older until their time comes to die.

What are the secrets to longevity through a good diet? Eating less has been found to be critical and seems to be the centre piece for longevity. A theory based on the diets of these long lived people has been doing the rounds for almost a century. In animal experiments, researchers have demonstrated that calorie restriction has now been clearly proven to be effective and up-to 30% calorie restriction leads to extended years in a manner believed to be similar to genetic modification. Additionally, high intake of vegetables, fruits, whole grains, soy, fish and eating less fat along with healthy lifestyle seems to explain protection from diseases and increased lifespan. Okinawan Cenetarian study reported that elder Okinawans who have attained the most phenomenal health and longevity daily eat an average of 7 servings of vegetables, 7 servings of whole grains, 2 servings of soy products; fish twice or thrice a week and very little sugar and added fats. Their diets include little meat and no margarines, hydrogenated fats or trans-fat. Although the impact of good nutrition on health and disease begins very early in life, it's never too late to make changes. According to researchers, at age 65 men and women in high-income countries still have a life expectancy of around 15 and 19 years respectively. The older one becomes, the longer one is likely to live, and thus, by the time men and women reach age 75, life expectancy is still 9 and 11 years, respectively. This dispels the common assumption that changes in lifestyle to improve health are no longer worthwhile in old age, and that the remaining years are insufficient to reap the benefits of dietary modifications. In fact, the prevalence of heart disease, diabetes, hypertension, obesity and arthritis is highest in the older population. Studies demonstrate that it is still worthwhile for older people to make lifestyle changes like diet modification, weight reduction, sodium restriction, saturated fat restriction smoking cessation - and that these changes make life in later years healthier, more active and less dependent.

The diets of the world's super-centenarians have a lot in common and here are recommendations based on their diets and lifestyles

• Eat less and eat well – low calories and nutrient dense foods.

• Choose a diet particularly rich in phyto-chemicals (antioxidants), vitamin B6, B12, folic acid, zinc, calcium, iron, chromium, vitamins D & E and omega-3 fats.

• Eat good carbohydrates, good fat, high quality proteins and fiber.

• Whole Food diets: include plenty of whole grains, fruits and vegetables.

• Prefer fresh, seasonal and locally grown organic foods.

• Include   protein rich foods such as fish, soy, legumes, peas and beans, seeds, nuts, fermented milk products, buttermilk and fermented foods.

• Natural sources of fats like seeds, nuts, olives, fish and cold pressed oils.

• Functional foods like barley, oats, soy, garlic, onion, mushrooms, berries, yogurt, olives, flax, nuts, herbs and spices.

• Some form of pro-biotic foods (good bacteria) like kefir (fermented milk), yogurt.

• Prebiotic foods (which promote growth of good bacteria) like whole grains, soy, vegetables, fruits and seeds.

• Limit intake of processed or refined foods, sugars, preservatives, chemicals etc.

• Avoid hydrogenated trans-fats.

• Occasionally indulge in celebration food - confectionery, desserts, sweets and candies.

• Eat regular meals, do not skip breakfast and eat dinners early.

• Eat smaller frequent meals.

• Ensure good sleep.

• Maintain regular physical activity throughout life.

Clearly, living long is not a coincidence. It is a result of many factors and when it comes to health and longevity, the sum of the dietary components is greater than its individual elements. The important thing to be remembered is that these scientifically proven secrets of the world's healthiest and long-lived people are simple to say the least – adopting them with common sense can certainly extend your later years with vibrancy and vitality.

IS PROTEIN EQUAL TO MUSCLE?

If you thought that eating proteins will help you build muscle, think again! Protein shakes, protein powders and supplements being pushed to unsuspecting ambitious youngsters in gyms with promises of biceps and triceps may do more harm than good. How much protein is really needed and are excesses safe, needs to be understood.

Many are under the impression that consuming high protein diet will increase muscle mass. The recommended daily allowance for protein is 0.8 g of protein per kg of body weight. Needs might be higher (1-1.5g/kg body weight) for periods of intense training, strength training (weight lifters, body builders) or weight restricted athletes, but there is little evidence that indicates a need for larger increases. Most athletes, assuming they eat a nutritionally balanced diet, have no need for extra protein except perhaps during periods of intense training.

Research suggests that the quantity of dietary protein needed to achieve maximal protein deposition is 1.5 g/ kg body weight and that the limiting factor for muscle protein deposition is energy intake, not protein. Therefore, athletes who wish to increase muscle mass should meet their energy (calorie) requirements first, through adequate intake of carbohydrates (60% of total calories), and then check that they have met their protein requirements. The fact is that it is weight training and not eating extra protein, is the key to building and strengthening muscle. The only way to build bigger, stronger muscles is to exercise them. To fuel heavy weight training, the body needs extra calories, especially from carbohydrates. According to recommendations, 500 kcals per day results in nearly half a kilogram increase in lean body weight per week during a resistance training programme.

Eating excessive amounts of protein, the extra calories will simply be stored (as fat) or burned. It can also lead to over-straining the kidneys and long-term metabolic problems

A balanced diet meeting caloric requirements with adequate servings of legumes, pulses, dairy, nuts or animal food meets the daily protein needs of most adults. It should also be noted that high protein diets containing meat and high fat dairy products may deliver an increased percentage of kilo-calories from fat. For this reason, athletes should be advised to select sources of high protein foods that contain low amounts of fat, such as skim milk, low fat yogurt, lean meats, fish and poultry, beans, legumes and egg whites.

Commercial supplements may be a convenient means for some busy athletes to secure additional protein in the diet. Many of these products contain high quality protein, such as milk, whey, egg or soy-protein; provide a balanced mixture of protein, carbohydrate, and fat for additional calories, and may also contain supplemental vitamins and minerals. Although these products do not contain all of the nutrients of natural foods, they may be useful adjuncts to a balanced diet.

Recommended protein intakes in grams per kilogram body weight for sedentary and physically active individuals

LECTINS

A relatively less talked about concept is the role of food as a messenger – carrying information and detailed instructions for every gene and every cell in the body. It enables them to repair, regenerate, restore, heal, harm or damage depending on what you eat. The word 'lectin' comes from the Latin word legere, meaning to pick out or to choose. This is exactly what lectins do – they are a type of protein that choose and bind with carbohydrates on cell membranes and form complexes (glycol-conjugates)on the membranes. These are present in most plants, especially seeds, nuts, cereals, legumes, beans, potatoes, tubers and dairy. They are also present in small amounts in some fruits, vegetables and seafood. Lectins are also present in the human body to some extent. Lectins, not to be confused with the endocrine hormone leptin, play a wide role in health – affecting immune function, cell growth, cell death and body fat regulation. Human lectins in our bodies act protectively as part of our immune system. However, lectins consumed in foods act as chemical.

Messengers and may cause gastrointestinal problems – cramping, bloating, flatulence, hyper-acidity, diarrhoea, nausea and vomiting. They are also implicated in food intolerances, inflammatory and auto-immune conditions. Other common manifestations of lectin-induced damage include skin rashes, joint pains and even increased urinary infections. Many food allergies are actually immune system reactions to lectins. Interestingly, lectins in food protect the seeds from micro-organisms, pests and insects. This is the reason why genetic modification of plants created a fluctuation in lectin content to develop pest resistant varieties. In our bodies, lectins are not digested and we create antibodies against them. Scientific literature shows that dietary lectins disrupt intestinal flora by reducing natural killer cells, and affect our health by causing inflammation. It is believed to contribute to leaky gut (thinning and increased permeability of the gut wall), inflammatory bowel disease (IBD), rheumatoid arthritis and even weight gain. The intestinal lining of people with Crohn's disease and IBS (irritable bowel syndrome) appears to be more sensitive to the effects of food lectins. Some lectins can be life threatening. They can cause death by clumping of red blood cells also called agglutination. For example, Ricin, a lectin from castor beans, even in minute amounts can cause massive clotting of red blood cells and death. Phytohaemagglutinin, a lectin in red kidney beans, is another dangerous lectin. Therefore, uncooked or raw sprouted red kidney beans should never be consumed. Another kind of lectin found in wheat called WGA (wheat germ agglutinin) has also been shown to interfere with protein digestion and increase gut permeability. Peanut lectin and soybean lectins are other examples of lectins. On the other hand, the lectins in jack-fruit, and common edible mushrooms, have been shown to slow the progression of colon cancer. Soaking, fermenting, sprouting and cooking helps in reducing lectins and increasing nutrient availability. Sprouting seeds, grains or beans decreases the lectin content. The longer the duration of sprouting, lower is the lectin content. It's no surprise that grandma never cooked beans without thoroughly washing and soaking. Fermentation allows beneficial bacteria to digest and degrade some lectins. No wonder traditional foods like idli, dosa, dhokla, sourdough bread, sauerkraut, kefir and yogurt are easy to digest for most people. Including friendly bacteria as in probiotics help in neutralising harmful effects of lectins, to some extent. Almost everybody has antibodies to some dietary lectins. Our diet and individual genetic inheritance determines how and to what degree lectins can affect us. It implies that we send the right signals and instructions through the right food to heal our cells. It's not therefore surprising that often we hear of several people getting cured of their chronic illnesses through simply changing the way they eat. The potential is huge and the right diet can help with common conditions like arthritis, fatigue, IBS, reflux, chronic allergies, eczema, psoriasis, autoimmune disease, diabetes, heart disease, migraines, depression, ADD, autism, and also help you lose weight without cravings, suffering and denial. Simple changes in the diet can thereby help treat chronic diseases.

MAGNESIUM

IMPORTANCE OF MAGNESIUM IN SPORTS / EXERCISE

Magnesium deficiency in our bodies is one of the most under-recognised deficiencies compared to other nutrients. A mineral which is widely available in our food supply and environment, seems to be causing serious concerns.

According to research published in March 2012 in Nutrition Reviews, more than half (56%) of the U.S. population consumed less than required amounts of magnesium from food in 2001-02, which corresponded to a sharp increase in type-2 diabetes in the U.S.

Magnesium plays an important role in energy production and storage, muscle contraction and maintenance of blood glucose levels and has been established as a key nutrient for all especially individuals with a regular exercise regimen and sports-persons. Magnesium is known to improve exercise, sports and athletic performance as it increases glucose availability as well as lactose clearance in the muscles during exercise. Magnesium is also known to promote strength and cardio-respiratory function in individuals. The role of magnesium among athletes appears to be far more significant than realised and can have life threatening consequences if overlooked.

Magnesium deficiency is associated with muscle weakness, cramps, structural damage of muscle fibers, strength and power limitation, therefore increasing susceptibility to cellular damage and affecting muscle performance.

Symptoms of magnesium deficiency include insomnia, muscle cramps, muscle weakness, headaches, fatigue, dizziness, irritability, hyper-excitability, decreased concentration and depression. Severe magnesium deficiency may cause low blood calcium and potassium levels, loss of appetite, nausea, arrhythmia (irregular heart beat), even cardiac arrest and sudden death.

Magnesium is lost through sweat and urine. Individuals engaged in intense exercise or exercising at high temperatures lose more magnesium than an average individual; hence their requirements are 10-20% higher than most individuals.

Accumulating evidence supports that sports individuals and people involved in regular exercise must pay special attention to their nutrient and micro-nutrient status. Recent surveys have revealed that most individuals, especially athletes, are unable to consume adequate levels of magnesium.

Magnesium deficiency is not only extremely common but is also linked to several diseases and health problems. But, many symptoms of low magnesium are not unique to magnesium deficiency alone, making it difficult to diagnose accurately. Blood or serum magnesium levels may not always reflect the true status. Therefore, low magnesium levels often go completely unrecognized and untreated.

Besides imbalanced diets (high in processed food and refined flours) magnesium deficiency is common among those suffering from chronic digestive problems, irritable bowel syndrome (IBS), crohn's, ulcerative colitis, mal-absorption, celiac disease, gluten-related disorders, endocrine problems, vitamin D deficiency, diabetes, chronic alcoholism, diuretics or among those who consume excess sugar or caffeine.

The mineral is found abundantly in foods like green vegetables, legumes, peas, beans and nuts (especially almonds), some shellfish and most whole un-refined cereals. Hard water has been found to contain more magnesium than soft water. Cooking decreases the magnesium content of food. There is experimental and clinical evidence that the amount of magnesium in urban and western diets is insufficient to meet individual needs and that magnesium deficiency may be contributing to common health problems. However, supplementation must be done under the care of a qualified professional.

FOOD DIARY

A Reality Check – Your Food Diary

Most of us live by beliefs and perceptions of 'what we eat'. Most overweight or obese people feel that they hardly eat. Many report eating only one or two breads (rotis) in the entire day. They seem to size up their entire food intake by these numerical counts.

Many focus on what they don't eat rather than what they eat. A great degree of denial seems to be apparent when it comes to acceptance of their food intake.

The first step to improve your diet is to increase awareness - what you eat, when you eat and how much you eat. Virtually a 'reality check' and there is nothing more powerful than a Food Diary. A simple objective tool helps you to track exactly what you really eat. Keeping a food diary for three days allows you to record everything you eat and drink. Adding details of the 'eating experience' makes it even more meaningful as 'what you eat' is often influenced by what's going on inside you and around you. So recording all this information can provide important insight into your eating patterns.

In a study, conducted by Harvard Medical School, researchers asked unsuccessful dieters to track what they ate. The dieters then ate exactly what they had listed. This time they all lost weight! A clear indicator of our subjective perceptions about 'what we eat'.

Food diary will show you whether you include all the food

groups in adequate amounts, the variety of foods you consume, the amount of sugar and undesirable foods; and the frequency of intake. After completing your food dairy, you can analyze the foods you've listed by comparing them to the five recommendations for healthy eating.

Don't be surprised if your food diary reveals that you're eating too many fats and too few fruits, vegetables, and grains. Remember – the food diary is a tool to help you. Don't use it to make yourself feel guilty or ashamed about your eating habits.

However, the validity of food diaries and self-reports is questionable for research. When researchers checked the validity of food diaries and self-reports, they found that obese people under reported their energy intake by 20-50% and lean people under reported by 10-30%.

In one study, researchers instructed participants to keep daily diaries of how much they ate and exercised for two weeks. Using accurate metabolic tests, researchers tracked the actual caloric intake and energy output of each participant. Participants underestimated their food intake and overestimated their energy output by about 50 percent.

In spite of this concern about accuracy, studies show that keeping a food diary was a better predictor of weight loss than were baseline body mass index, exercise and age. Writing down everything you eat is a powerful technique. It tells you where the calories are coming from and helps to develop specific plans to deal with those situations. In addition, a food diary helps hold dieters accountable for what they are eating. It is not surprising then that a food diary has considerable 'power as a predictor of success in achieving weight loss'.

A study involving 1,685 middle–aged men and women over six months found those who kept such a diary lost about twice as much weight as those who did not.

A food diary also helps in diet related conditions like allergies, irritable bowel syndrome (IBS) and during pregnancy. They can also be used to identify those at risk of under-nutrition and monitor those on nutritional support. It can be used for nutrition education and for achieving dietary goals for sports persons etc.

So, while a food diary heightens awareness, to be useful, it must be kept with care. Be accurate and list everything you eat as soon as you can! If possible, record what you eat as you eat it. Be specific about portion size and foods that contain more than one ingredient. For example, if you eat a sandwich, list the kind of sandwich and the portion size of the bread. Don't forget to mention the butter or mayonnaise or that extra slice of cheese. The longer you wait to record what you eat, the less accurate you'll be. However, even if it is not done formally, scribbling down what you're eating can help a great deal.

You may also want to consider using your food diary for longer periods to monitor your diet and manage or maintain your weight. It can help you identify problems in your diet, improve it and reduce risk of diet related conditions.

So, next time you resolve to improve your diet, start by reaching out for a pen and a paper. It works like that mirror on the wall!

HEALTHY COOKWARE

It's important to understand the difference between the materials and how they affect us in order to make the best choices.

• Common cookware material includes cast iron, copper, brass, bronze, stainless steel, aluminium, and Teflon.

• Cast iron cookware is heavy, inexpensive and doesn't rust easily. The conduction of heat is slow and even; thus making it best for use when cooking in the stove or oven. Cooking utensils such as frying pans, saucepans and sometimes kettles are also made out of this material. Food cooked in iron vessels enhances the iron content substantially. The more acidic the food, the higher the iron content. It has been reported that the iron content of pasta sauce cooked in an iron vessel increases by about 300%. This makes cooking in iron pots and pans highly desirable, particularly in India, where anemia is a major public health problem. Some simple traditional treatment done to the pan can turn it into a non-stick surface.

• Copper and its alloys brass and bronze have been in use for a long time. Brass is an alloy of copper and zinc, while bronze is an alloy of copper and tin.

• Copper (tamba) and brass (peetal) have been used traditionally for cooking. They are not too heavy and are good conductors of heat and distribute heat evenly. However, they are easy to tarnish and reactive to acids and salt. Tarnish, if gets into food, can cause food poisoning. Organic acids from food can lead to excessive copper in food, which can be deterimental to health. Therefore, they must be coated with tin (kalai). Tinning should be pure, strong and should not be contaminated with lead – a deadly poison. However, being soft, the tin coating wears off rapidly with the constant scrubbing and cleaning and requires periodic renewal. This makes the use of properly-tinned copper and brass vessels safe for cooking but cumbersome. Periodic tinning also makes them expensive in the long run.

• Bronze, though, is heavy and strong, it is brittle and can break easily if it falls. Being costly too, its use is restrictive.

• Aluminium cookware is light, strong, corrosion resistant, conducts heat well and is inexpensive. This has lead to its immense popularity as a cooking ware in homes and commercial kitchens. Pressure cookers, a must in every home are made from this metal. However, aluminium is an extremely soft and reactive metal. Contact with strong acids, alkalies and salt from food causes the metal to dissolve forming pits. Also, vigorous stirring and scrubbing during washing causes the metal to wear off. Often boiling tomatoes, tamarind, vinegar and acidic dishes like sambhar causes the metal to dissolve rapidly, tending to affect the taste of food.

• Presence of aluminium in our diet has been reported to be a serious concern. Aluminium can inhibit absorption of important minerals like iron and calcium. It may also accumulate in bones leading to 'de-mineralization' (softening) of bones. Aluminium deposits have also been found in brain tissue of patients suffering from Alzheimer's disease, a progressive neuro-degenerative disorder associated with dementia. Therefore, despite its apparent utility as a cookware, the use of aluminium must be avoided. Also, avoid storing acidic food like tea, tomato puree, sambhar, chutneys etc. in aluminium pots.

- Stainless steel cookware has replaced iron, copper and aluminium in a big way owing to its attributes including its strength, high durability, rust proof, low cost of maintenance and easy handling. However, stainless steel is not a good conductor of heat and may develop hot spots, darken or may cause food to burn due to uneven heat distribution. This disadvantage has been overcome by the use of copper bottom stainless steel. This cookware made from stainless steel sheets with layer copper on the bottom for quick and better heat conductivity prevents food from burning. Stainless steel cookware is safe and effective, although it may be expensive.

- Non-stick cookware, the modern housewife has switched to teflon coated non-stick cookware for several reasons. Besides, cutting back on fat consumption drastically and not allowing food to stick on the pan, non-stick cookware is easy to clean. However, some concerns regarding PFOAs (perfluoroctanoicacid-suspected human carcinogen) associated with non-stick cookware have been raised. Break on the surface due to scratching, misuse or overheating may release harmful compounds. Therefore, do not overheat the pans, do not leave pans unattended on stoves, or use metal utensils on the non-stick coating, which scrape off the finish. Do not use abrasive cleaners or stack the pans one on top of the other and always use wooden spatulas. In other words, follow manufacturers' instructions carefully.

Storing highly acidic or salty foods such as tomato sauce, sambhar or chutneys in aluminum pots may cause more aluminum than usual to enter the food than recommended.

These foods will also cause pitting on the pot's surface. During cooking, aluminum dissolves most easily from worn or pitted pots and pans. The longer food is cooked or stored in aluminum, the greater the amount that gets into food. Acidic foods, such as tomatoes and citrus products, absorb the most aluminum.

Hard Anodized Aluminium: Anodizing is an electro-chemical process that hardens aluminium making it non-stick, scratch-resistant, durable and easy to clean, It seals the aluminum, preventing any reaction to acidic foods and leaching of aluminum into food. Anodized aluminium conducts heat as well as ordinary aluminum and is reported to be harder than steel. It is chemically stable, does not decompose and is non-toxic, unlike regular aluminium pans. The surface remains smooth and does not pit. Being hard and smooth, it minimizes sticking of food and allows uniform heating.

Ceramic pottery is porous and unsafe, unfit for cooking unless glazed. These glazes resist wear and tear, discoloration and corrosion. Poor quality, locally produced cheap glazes can be a source of metals like lead and cadmium and lead to lead and cadmium poisoning. Glazes that are approved for use are safe and can be used to cook and store.

Enamel: Enamel-coated iron and steel is colourful, stain and scratch-resistant and does not pick up food odours. With proper care, a fine enamel pot lasts a lifetime, whereas an enamel cookware with a thin enamel layer that chips easily can be harmful to health.

Microwave plastics: Often, stories about the dangers of chemicals leaching from plastic into micro-waved food have circulated.

Consumers need to know the following safety rules for microwave cooking:

• Cook only in containers labeled for use in the microwave.

• Leave a gap between food and plastic wrap.

• Consider waxed paper safe. If you use paper towels, choose the plain white kind, not coloured.

• Don't use recycled tubs or take-away containers in the microwave. They aren't heat-tested, and could allow chemicals to leach into food and may be serious health hazards.

• Avoid visibly damaged, stained or unpleasant smelling plastics and containers.

Microwaves are commonly used since 1970s. Concerns regarding their safety and health implications are rising. Although the regulatory health authorities consider it safe, if instructions are followed correctly.

Some studies have shown health concerns relating to its radiations and others to its nutritional aspect. Its well documented that nutritional value of microwaved food is preserved effectively, may be better than conventional cooking. However, losses of certain essential nutrients like antioxidants, flavanoid, vitamins like vitamin B12 and other phenolic compounds have been reported. One of the studies have reported higher losses of flavonoids (97%), sinapic acid derivatives (74%) and caffeoyl-quinic acid derivatives (87%) in broccoli, when it was microwaved compared to conventional cooking methods. It is suggested that minimum addition of water during cooking of vegetables will be helpful in preventing these losses.

Till further research evidence is gathered, it is suggested that microwaves are used with care, not as an alternative to conventional cooking and are better used for reheating.

Microwave Musts:

• Don't operate an oven if the door does not close firmly or is bent, warped, or otherwise damaged.

• As an added safety precaution, don't stand directly against an oven (and don't allow children to do this) for long periods of time while it is operating. Pregnant women must take special care.

• Do not heat water or liquids in the microwave oven for excessive amounts of time.

Over-heating of water in a cup can result in superheated water (water heated past its boiling temperature), which does not appear to be boiling. If super-heating has occurred, a slight disturbance or movement such as picking up the cup, or pouring in a spoon full of instant coffee, may result in a violent eruption with the boiling water exploding out of the cup.

• To ensure uniform heating, turn the dish several times during cooking.

• Stir soups and stews periodically during reheating to ensure even heating.

• Remove food from packaging before defrosting. Do not use foam trays and plastic wraps because they are not heat stable at high temperatures. Melting or warping may cause harmful chemicals to migrate into food.

EATING WITH EYES

Eyes are bigger than our stomach / Eyeball eating / The see food diet. Most of us would decline if offered to eat right after a meal, yet if something tempting is brought in front of us, we would reach out for it! External cues are often hidden and are known to influence our appetite and have very little to do with hunger. These include family, friends, packages and plates, names and numbers, labels and lights, colours and candles, shapes and smell, distractions and distances, cupboards and containers. Visual cues are very powerful drivers to eating and determine how much we eat.

One of the strongest psychological motivators to eat more than what we should, seems to be the need to empty our plates. The need to finish all that is on the plate from our childhood and the dislike of waste drives us to eating regardless of our hunger. Don't let anyone put you on a guilt trip about hunger in Somalia and poor children. Don't worry about leaving a morsel on your plate when pleasantly full.

Also, the larger the portion, the more we eat; the bigger the container, the more we pour. It takes about twenty minutes before the brain gets the signal that the stomach is full; meaning that if you eat fast in less than twenty minutes, then the sensation that the belly is full will arrive too late, likely to make you eat more than you need. So eat slowly and pay attention to what you eat and stop when you are eighty percent full. Put your spoon or fork down between each bite. Ask yourself whether you are hungry rather than wait to be full. The 'not hungry' situation happens earlier and that's when you must stop.

When eating out, if portions are large, don't hesitate to ask the waiter to pack some of it before it reaches the table. For the same reasons, don't stock undesirable food around the house. Don't store undesirable food in transparent containers.

In some cases, looking at food can make you eat less. If you are presented with an indication of how much you have already eaten, perhaps by wrappers, bottles and bones or by 'pre-plating' your food or even with your food diary, you may be surprised to find that you will end up eating less.

Understanding why we eat the way we do, we can eat a little less, eat healthier and enjoy it a lot more. Take control of subtle influences in our environment that can persuade us to eat or overeat. How small changes in our daily habits can contribute to reducing our expanding girth is amazing.

Take 5

- Don't worry about plate waste, think about your waist.
- Eat slowly. Stop eating before you are 80 percent full.
- Use smaller plates, bowls and glasses.
- Pre-plate your food.
- Control your portions.

Use the hunger scale to address what you eat, when you eat, how you eat and when to stop?

Hunger scale

Follow the hunger scale to help you eat when you are hungry and stop when you should be stopping.

- Physically faint
- Ravenous

- Fairly hungry
- Slightly hungry
- Neutral
- Pleasantly satisfied
- Full
- Stuffed
- Bloated
- Nauseous

Eat when you are fairly or slightly hungry and stop when you are pleasantly full.

HOW TO FIGHT JET LAG?

How to minimize the jet lag?

Jet lag is the desire to sleep during the daytime, inability to sleep at night, feeling of general fatigue, irritability, loss of appetite and inability to perform routine activities due to lack of concentration after a flight across several time zones. The middle aged and the elderly with a regular life style are worst affected. Those who are generally not able to have a restful sleep may also suffer from severe jet lag. Jet lag tends to hit harder during travel towards East than after a Westward flight. This is because a flight towards East shortens the day while a flight in the Western direction makes the day longer. Adaptation to the latter is easier.

It generally takes several days to adjust to the new time zone, generally half to one day for each time zone crossed. Sometimes, jet lag appears one or two days after reaching the destination. This may be due to sleep deprivation during flight, which initially leads to a good sleep.

Why Does jet lag Occur?

Every human being has an internal (biological) clock that sets an individual's time for sleeping, waking, eating and other bodily functions in a 24 hours period. During long distance air travel, several time zones are crossed rapidly. On arrival, the resulting day is either longer or shorter than 24 hours, depending on the direction of flight. Therefore the usual pattern of sleeping and waking is disturbed. For example, if you board a 10 pm flight from New Delhi, it will arrive at Singapore in the early morning hours while it is still night in Delhi. Since your biological system is tuned to Delhi, you may feel sleepy for a few hours on arrival at Singapore and then be unable to sleep during the night. After a day or two, your sleep-wake cycle will reset itself. Till such time, your internal clock will remain non-synchronous with local time and you may continue to feel tired and your efficiency may drop.

How to prevent jet lag?

The only sure way to combat jet lag is to rough it out. Yet, attention to a simple plan of action may help to minimize this problem. The preparation should begin about a week or more before the flight.

Preparation for the flight:

• Adjust your bedtime for a week prior to the journey. When flying west, try to sleep slightly late. For an eastward flight, bedtime should be preponed. There should be a gradual shift in the bedtime, say 10 minutes earlier or later every alternate day.

• If possible, plan to reach your destination in the evening so that you may retire early to bed.

• Keep a short acting sleeping pill in your travel bag.

During the flight:

• After boarding the aircraft, reset the watch to the local time or your destination. From then on, perform your in-flight activities according to the time displayed on your watch.

• Try to sleep till the breakfast time of your destination.

• Turn off your seat light and draw the curtain if possible when sleeping.

• Keep awake during normal waking hours of your destination.

• Intermittently take a short walk in the plane during waking hours.

• Try to use a bright and focused source of light for reading.

• If possible, break a long journey and rest at night in between.

• Drink adequate quantity of non-alcoholic drinks like fruit juices. Air in jet planes is dry.

• Avoid alcohol and heavy meals. Eat a high protein, low fat breakfast, a high protein lunch, and a high carbohydrate dinner.

After the flight:

• Go to sleep early if you arrive at your destination during evening time. Take a sleeping pill to induce sleep if needed.

• If you reach your destination in the morning or afternoon, spend your time outdoors to ensure adequate exposure to sunlight. Exposure to bright sunlight for more than 6 hours at a stretch may adjust you to new time zone within 2-3 days instead of 5-15 days.

The anti jet lag diet:

A diet developed by Charles Ehret of U.S. is claimed to minimize jet lag by resetting the internal clock of the body to the new time zone (Table).

Medicines for jet lag:

Recently, attention has been focused on the possible role of melatonin in prevention of jet lag. Melatonin is a hormone, which plays a crucial role in control of internal clock of the body. Its secretion is stimulated by darkness and suppressed by light.

It has been claimed that an injection of melatonin before a trans-meridian journey may synchronize the sleep and waking pattern with local time of the destination. It may synchronize other functions of the internal clock too, leading to a rapid adaptation to the new place. These claims are currently under investigation. Till such time the results of trials with melatonin are available, it is better to use a low dose of a sleeping pill to induce sleep after a long distance flight across several time zones. However, the pill should be taken at or shortly before bedtime, and not for inducing sleep in the daytime. Sleeping in the day after arrival may slow down recovery from jet lag. Moreover, the sleeping pill should be short acting so that it neither leaves hangover nor successive doses have a cumulative effect on the sleep.

The anti jet lag diet

3 days before flight

• Eat a high protein breakfast and lunch of beans, cottage cheese, milk, eggs (feast schedule), fish and poultry.

- Eat a high carbohydrate dinner of rice, bread, potatoes and sweet desserts.
- Avoid caffeinated drinks except between 3 pm to 5 pm.

2 days before Flight
- Eat a low calorie, low carbohydrate, low protein diet consisting (fast schedule) of vegetables, fruits, soups, juices and salads.
- Caffeinated drinks may be taken between 3 pm to 5 pm.

1 day before flight:
- Observe feast schedule

On the day of Flight
- Observe fast schedule

On flight:
- Take a high protein breakfast and lunch and a high carbohydrate dinner, but watch your calorie intake.

HOLIDAYS

Vacation is meant to recharge your energies, rewind and refocus, so that you are refreshed to return to routine and cope with work pressures. However, how you treat yourself on a vacation determines whether this becomes a reality. More often than not, I find people over-indulging in food and drinks, off from exercise schedules on the pretext of being on a holiday. This makes people not only gain weight but also makes them feel sluggish and tired.

According to studies, most people gain approximately one to two kilograms every holiday season. Research shows that extra weight often gained during the holidays tends to build up over the years, contributing to long-term obesity.

• Be active – If you exercise regularly, don't stop – continue to exercise over the holidays. If a holiday party includes dancing, join in! Check if the hotel you book has a gym, or else go for walks, run, swim, play sports or cycle outdoors.

• Choose one favourite meal for the day and plan other meals accordingly. The other meals could be light around salads, vegetables and soups. Breakfast buffets can throw you off, so plan to eat appropriately.

• If you are very keen on desserts then either try a bite or if you want a full portion just take a very light meal.

• Schedule feasting times – If possible, schedule holiday dinners at normal meal times. Having meals outside of normal meal times contributes to overeating, particularly, large meals late into the night.

• Carry appropriate snack food to munch like seeds, roasted nuts or whole grains so you are not forced to buy unhealthy stuff off the shelf.

• Watch your drinks – Avoid sweetened beverages, fruit juices, mock-tails and cocktails. It is best to drink water whenever possible. Diet beverages made with artificial sweeteners can help control calories at celebrations, although drinking them on a regular basis may not help with long-term weight control.

• Count your alcohol – Alcohol can be a major source of hidden calories as well. I know several patients who say they can manage their food on a holiday but not alcohol and some also manage to finish a bottle of wine in one evening.

A single shot of liquor, about 30 ml, is nearly 125 calories. A 150 ml glass of wine or a 350 ml glass of beer is about 160. Sweet mixed drinks have even more calories. 250 ml margarita, for example, has 240 calories. Ginger ale has 120 calories. Beer guzzling too can be dangerous. Simple things like having a tomato juice rather than a Bloody Mary can help.

• Food choices - Choose foods that are lower in energy density, meaning they have fewer calories for their size. You'll feel fuller soon and take in fewer calories. For example, start out your meal with a salad or soup. Skip the second helpings of oily gravies, fried food and breads. Ask for vegetables instead of potatoes or fries. Having a fibre supplement pre-meal is useful to cut back on richer food later.

• Eat healthy snacks before a special dinner – Eating a snack like fruit/ nuts/milk/yoghurt helps to avoid overeating at a big holiday dinner. Also, use smaller plates when they're available – bigger plates encourage taking larger food portions and eating larger quantities of food than small plates.

Some checks and balances, while you enjoy yourself are all that are needed to avoid gaining those extra kilos and making the most of your vacation. Following a few simple healthy habits the next time you holiday can go a long way to energize you and save you from gaining the extra kilos.

STAYING WELL WHEN YOU TRAVEL

• Before you travel, check with your physician, medicines to be carried when traveling.

- Always wash your hands with soap and water or use a hand sanitizer before handling food or eating.
- Eat only cooked and canned foods. Eat raw fruits and vegetables, only if you have washed them thoroughly. As far as possible, skip salads.
- Be aware that water, ice and beverages made from water and milk may be unsafe. Drink only if you are sure of the quality of milk and water. Try having beverages without ice.
- If you suspect the quality of local water, use disinfected or boiled water even for brushing your teeth.
- In general, remember these rules: boil it, cook it, peel it, or forget it.

Fighting/ Prevent Holiday Weight Gain

Be it a cruise, hill holidays or beach vacation, most people end up gathering extra kilos after a holiday. Feeling sluggish, sloppy, sleepy and tired, as a result of over indulgence in food and drink are common. A relaxed mind and plenty of good food and wine can take its toll. Also, recognizing the potential long term effects that holiday weight gain can have on your body is important. Excessive weight can lead to health problems such as diabetes, heart disease and high blood pressure. Gaining unnecessary kilos now, makes it harder to lose weight later.

SITTING

STAND UP FOR HEALTH

While poor diet stands to be the biggest risk factor for chronic diseases, physical inactivity is an important independent factor.

Exercise can keep off and at times even reverse diseases both mental and physical. According to studies regular modest exercise helps mild cognitive decline, boosts immune system, improves blood pressure, blood sugars, hormonal disorders, mood, digestive health, sleep quality and reduces excess body weight among others. Body weight and physical inactivity together are estimated to account for one third of common cancers like breast, colon, endometrium, kidney and oesophagus. However, those with high pressure jobs or with long sitting demands find it hard to keep to exercise schedules. The problem appears to be the sedentary 'sitting', independent of exercise.

Tracking the health of more than hundred thousand persons in the US for fourteen years the American Cancer Society study found that men who sit for six or more hours per day have a 20 percent higher over all death rate compared to men who sit for three hours or less. Worse still women who sit more than six hours have a 40 percent higher death rate. In fact a meta analysis of 43 such studies found that excess sitting was associated with a shorter life span and interestingly this is "regardless of physical activity level". Simply said even those who hit the gym after work may still have shortened life spans if they continue to sit all day! Sitting more than six hours has indeed increased mortality even among regular runners or swimmers. According to some studies more than three hours (180 minutes) of sitting increases diabetes risk by three fold.

One of the ways sitting can be so harmful to health is circulation through damage to the inner walls of arteries. Also called endothelial dysfunction wherein the arteries do not relax enough to allow blood flow. This leads to arterial dysfunction which eventually can cause blockages and lead to poor circulation in the limbs. Gradually the risk increases for almost all chronic diseases. So all in all the goal is not to give up working or working out but ensure you do not sit for too long at a stretch.

1) Add 10 / 15 minutes walk a few times a day. Try to use the stairs as much as possible rather than elevators.

2) Try to stand even while working if possible. A stand up desk or taking the stairs a few times or opting for 'walking meetings' instead of sit down ones are easy options.

3) Regular getting up for a minute or two are enough. Get your own tea / coffee and find reasons to move around at work or at home.

4) Yet there may be those who just have to sit as a part of their job. These could be pilots, drivers etc. Such people must ensure that they reduce the burden of other risk factors. They must not smoke or be obese. They should boost their levels of antioxidants through fruits, vegetables, several cups of green tea, turmeric, green leafy vegetables, berries etc. They must also add regular physical activity to their routine. Needless to say increased physical exercise outside of the work routine is critical.

5) Have regular health checks and take care of nutritional deficiencies.

6) Try to achieve the goal of ten thousand steps a day

regardless of what your job is. While treadmill desks are not an option yet for most the above tips are sure to save you the risks of sitting at work or at home.

CARB WISE

Carbohydrates have earned a bad reputation among weight watchers. These are not bad, as not all carbohydrates are equal, what matters is how one chooses them. That is some may be healthier than others. Carbohydrates are a macro-nutrient found in many common foods. Plant based foods such as grains and pulses (dals and legumes) are rich in carbohydrates. Commercially prepared, packed and processed foods may have added sugar or starch, which are forms of carbohydrates. Carbohydrate in its simplest form is sugar or glucose while in its complex form it is found as starch. Fiber is also a form of indigestible carbohydrate. Carbohydrates have numerous health benefits and have an important role in our diets. These include providing energy, protecting against diseases and weight control. The body uses carbohydrates as its main fuel. Sugars and starches are broken down into simple sugars during digestion and are absorbed in the bloodstream. Some of this is used as fuel for activity and excess is converted to fat.

Carbohydrates increase blood sugars and can be classified on the basis of their effect on blood sugars. This is measured in a frequently used term called 'glycemic index'.

Besides quality, amount of carbohydrates too is important. According to recommendations, carbohydrates make up 45 to

60% of our total daily calories. So choose carbohydrates wisely. Go for whole grains like barley, oats, brown rice, legumes, dals, soybean, fruits, vegetables, low fat dairy, nuts and seeds. Limit foods with added sugars and refined grains, fruit juices, sweetened drinks, desserts and candy.

RAW VS COOKED VEGETABLES

Whether vegetables are beneficial raw or cooked has been the subject of debate and much interest. That raw food and cooked food might affect the body differently was proposed as early as in the 1930s, when Dr Kouchakoff presented his work on feeding experiments in humans at the First International Congress of Microbiology.

Evidence suggests that cooking vegetables has some harmful effects, as it destroys certain nutrients and enzymes. However, cooking helps by killing potentially harmful organisms and increasing safety but also actually improves the bioavailability of certain nutrients and improves digestibility.

The truth is that vegetables are beneficial in both raw and cooked state. Cooking vegetables decreases water-soluble and eat-sensitive nutrients, such as vitamin C, B-vitamins and folic acid. It also showed that higher levels for these nutrients among salad consumers suggested better absorption. In fact, it was reported that salad and raw vegetable consumption has been found to be positively associated with higher levels of these nutrients among adults in the U.S. population.

Some enzymes too are destroyed by heat. Garlic and cruciferous vegetables, which include cauliflower, broccoli and brussel sprouts, contain special enzymes with anti-cancer properties. However, heating these vegetables destroys these properties. At times, increasing cooking time and temperatures of vegetables creates some harmful by-products called dietary advanced glycation end products (AGEs). AGEs in our food are irritants which can lead to several disorders including allergies, digestive disorders, arthritis, asthma, inflammation, aches and pains and accelerate ageing.

In addition to loss of nutrients, enzyme activity and formation of AGEs, cooking vegetables is likely to affect their glycemic indices. Glycemic index is the ability of carbohydrates in food to raise blood sugar levels. As the digestibility improves, the carbohydrate availability also increases. This means quicker increase in sugar and insulin (hormone which favours hunger and belly fat). Therefore, raw vegetables work more favourably for weight watchers and diabetics.

Another factor is that most vegetables when taken raw leave an alkaline ash which helps in better absorption of several nutrients. In fact, raw vegetables have been found to be strongly associated with protection against cancer, particularly esophageal, gastric, and breast cancers.

While there are losses during cooking in some instances, cooking has some positive effects too. Besides making it safer, cooking vegetables increases bioavailability of vitamin A. A study found that heating tomatoes resulted in significantly increased lycopene content and antioxidant activity despite a decrease in vitamin C. Studies of colorectal cancer showed both raw and cooked vegetables to be inversely associated with risk. To conclude eat at least 50 percent of vegetables raw and fifty percent cooked.

But by no means over-cook vegetables. Remember, however, that salads, vegetable juices and raw vegetables and fruits can be a source of infection and must be consumed only where highest levels of hygiene are maintained.

A note on carbohydrate:

Carbohydrates, or carbs, are commonly used as a synonym for grains or cereals like rice, roti, pasta or breads. The question that most people ask is that if you don't eat roti or rice then where does the daily intake of carbohydrates come from? The answer is that even dairy, fruits and dals contribute to some amount of carbohydrates in our diets. Common sources of naturally occurring carbohydrates include fruits, vegetables, dairy, grains, legumes, sugars, honey, jaggery etc. They have low glycemic index carbohydrates, which take longer to release sugars in the blood and keep us fuller for a longer duration.

They are suitable for dieters, weight and waist watchers. Vegetables too have small amounts of carbohydrates, especially starchy vegetables like potatoes, sweet potato and colocassia (arbi). These starchy vegetables if taken in sizable quantities or had regularly are counted as carbohydrates. You should steer clear of conventional staples or cereals to get your carbohydrates. They can be totally avoided, but only under professional guidance. Cereals can be substituted by pulses, lentils, nut flours in the form of pancakes and chillas. Those who wish to be stricter can include sprouts in their diets. Sprouts also have other benefits in the form of enzymes and higher nutrition.

Grains or cereals preferable should be consumed by 7.00–7.30 pm. Grains or cereals can be had with proteins or vegetables or both – roti or rice with dal or vegetables with egg, lean meat, fish or yogurt, cottage cheese. For your non-cereal meals, have dals or lentils with vegetables or salads. Multi-grain or nut flours work better, especially when watching your carb intake and calories.

ALL ABOUT FRUITS

If you thought going on a fruit diet will help you lose your flab, think again! Undisputedly fruits and vegetables are central to a weight loss diet and good health. However, recent research suggests that excessive intake of sugar from fruits can be harmful. Sugar from fruits, also called fructose, in excessive amounts (>50gms / day) can be counter-productive for many and can increase the risk of obesity, diabetes and heart disease.

Fructose is a simple sugar that is present in fruits, fruit juices and honey. It is responsible for their sweet taste. Besides fruits, a significant source of fructose in our diets is table sugar (sucrose), which is made up of 50% fructose and 50% glucose. Sweetened beverages and fruit juices contribute significantly to high fructose intake in the urban diet worldwide leading to extra pounds in tricky ways and in part explains the growing epidemic of obesity and diabetes. Unlike other sugars like glucose, ingestion of excessive fructose is associated with insulin resistance leading to metabolic syndrome – a constellation of factors including increased blood sugar levels, high triglycerides, high uric acid, fat deposition in the liver (fatty liver) and weight gain, particularly around the belly. Other complications associated with metabolic syndrome include high blood pressure, endothelial dysfunction (damage to lining of blood vessels), increased oxidative stress, increased inflammation, increased intra-abdominal fat accumulation (appetite controlling hormone). These eventually increase the risk to obesity, type-2 diabetes, heart disease and other chronic diseases.

High fructose intake causes fat to accumulate in the blood and liver. Instead of being used immediately for energy, the fructose is readily converted into triglycerides (blood fats) by the liver. According to the National Institute of Health (United States), the growing incidence of gout, due to high uric acid levels also coincides with a substantial increase in the consumption of soft drinks containing fructose.

Researchers found that when overweight individuals were fed equal calories from glucose and fructose, both sugars caused about the same degree of weight gain, but an important difference in the nature of these gains was evident. The fructose group gained more fat in their abdominal area which is known to elevate the risk of diabetes and heart disease to a greater degree than fat stored elsewhere in the body.

The ability of fructose to induce insulin resistance can be shown with diets as low as 15–25% fructose. So, next time when you go on that 'fruit diet', watch your portions.

A prudent approach to fruit intake must be maintained. In general, enjoy the pleasures of sweets within limits. Empty calories from sweetened drinks, punches, cocktails and fruit juices will do well to be replaced by water, plain soda, coconut water, kokum juice, butter milk or vegetable juices.

There is an urgent need for increased public awareness of the risks associated with high fructose consumption and greater efforts should be made to curb the addition of high fructose additives to packaged foods.

Selected References

https://jamanetwork.com/journals/jamaotolaryngology/
fullarticle/2675082

https://academic.oup.com/ajcn/article/70/6/1040/4729179

https://pubs.acs.org/doi/abs/10.1021/ja01543a060

https://journals.sagepub.com/doi/pdf/10.1177/088
3073809351315

https://www.hindawi.com/journals/jobe/2011/

ACKNOWLEDGMENTS

First and foremost, I thank my publisher Simon & Schuster and Dharini who approached me for doing this book. A special book for the office worker sounded so niche but on giving it a deeper thought, I was convinced of its relevance and need. I would like to thank Sayantan, Rahul and Himanjali who worked tirelessly to make this book possible. A special thanks to my co-author Nina Mehta, who helped me put my thoughts and words to paper and get started. Always in gratitude to my dear daughters, Gayatri and Ishita, who are integral to whatever I do and without whose support I can never do anything. They are selfless human beings and I wish them the best always. I would also like to mention the contribution of all my office staff, specially Shivani, who helped with the writing and compilation of the manuscript. She has been a quiet worker and manages my office almost seamlessly.

The recipes included in this book are a collection of some of my own along with contributions by friends, family, patients and Veenaji. A special contributor is chef Aarman Kler. The young man has combined the essence of the book with his creative genius to produce some truly exciting yet simple recipes. You are sure to enjoy them. A big thank you and blessing to Aarman.

I would be incomplete if I did not mention my family's support including my beloved husband Gagan, my dearest sons, Karan Vir and Dev Aditya, who allowed me to work as they supported and balanced other parts of my life; my nephews, Vahin and Yuv, who coined the title of the book. A very special thanks to my dearest mother for making me who I am. Last but not the least, a special thanks to all my family and friends who have not been mentioned by name but have played an important role in shaping my career; I must mention my friends, Devendra Bhatnagar (Bhutto), Dr Divya Prasher and Anu Kler who graciously helped with thier skills when ever I needed. I thank my patients for having faith in me and having trusted me with their lives. They are instrumental in my reaching where I am today. In gratitude.

ABOUT THE AUTHORS

Ishi Khosla is a practicing clinical nutritionist, consultant, writer, columnist, researcher, author and entrepreneur. She is actively involved in clinical practice at the Centre for Dietary Counselling in Delhi, and has spearheaded the first of its kind health food company 'Whole Foods India'. An author of multiple books, including The Diet Doctor and Is Wheat Killing You? Ishi has also been listed among the twenty-five most powerful women in the country by the India Today Group. Besides this, she has been nominated as a member of the Programme Advisory Committee, Doordarshan Kendra; is a member of the Governing Body of Lady Irwin College, Delhi University; and is a consultant to several organizations. She is the founder of The Celiac Society of India. Ishi lives in New Delhi.

Nina Mehta is a content writer and news reporter, spanning business journalism at News Mobile, Dew Jones Newswires and Hindustan Times and providing editorial content solutions to corporates like ABC Consulting, Genpact, Strategic Communications & PR and Your Nest Angel Investors.

Chef Aarman Kler (Recipes contributed by him) is passionate about food and started experimenting with ingredients from different cuisines at an early age. He is able to innovate, blend flavours and produces unique and creative dishes. An alumnus of Modern School Barakhamba Road and student of Economics at the Simon Fraser University, he honed his talent by studying the culinary arts further in Vancouver and the Intensive Culinary Arts Programme (ICAP) at the Indian School of Hospitality. Aarman has worked at an array of world famous restaurants. His recipes are healthy, minimalist and intriguing to the palette.

A NOTE ON WHOLE FOODS

'Whole Foods' was founded by Ms Ishi Khosla, a practicing clinical nutritionist (and author of this book) in 2001. Whole Foods was an effort to restore balance in today's skewed diets. In the prevalent fast paced urban lifestyles, most people find it difficult to eat healthy and nutritious food and engage in adequate physical activity. This resulted in increase in several lifestyle related diseases. Obesity, type II diabetes and heart disease and food allergies have assumed epidemic proportions in our country.

Several nutrition concerns have been addressed through Whole Foods. Commercially available conventional foods have high calorie content, high fat, trans fats (harmful artery-clogging fats), excessive chemicals and preservatives coupled with high carbohydrates, sugar and glycemic load. Worse still, they are low in protective constituents like fiber, essential fats, vitamins, minerals and anti-oxidants.

Whole Foods helps people to make healthy food choices, which are easily available, convenient without compromising on taste. Products that are high on nutrition and lower in calories, free of toxic ingredients like trans-fats, artificial preservatives and colours. It incorporates functional foods, healthy fats, whole grains including brown rice, nuts, seeds, honey, jaggery and a variety of fresh vegetables and fruits to promote health and wellbeing.

Whole Foods is also a conscientious and major manufacturer of an extensive range of gluten free products, including bakery. With its extensive precautions, state of the art in-house lab under the supervision of food technologists and microbiologists, the wheat intolerant patient has access to safe food.

The rising awareness and response to healthy eating has been encouraging. The endeavour continues to be to not only provide the best but also to educate the public through various awareness programmes. A recent development has been that m/s Haldiram Manufacturing Pvt.Ltd (Delhi), the largest snack food manufacturer in the country, has acquired major shareholding to give Whole Foods fiscal strength and business reach to spread the approach of good, nutritious and healthy food across the globe.